International Relations 1918 - 1939

The Versailles Peace Treaties, the League
of Nations, Hitler's foreign policy & the
causes of the Second World War

A H Goddard

ISBN-13: 978-1985251694
ISBN-10: 1985251698

Contents

The Versailles Peace Treaties

The League of Nations

Hitler's foreign policy and appeasement

Revision Tracking List

Time line

1918	Armistice - End of First World War
1919	Treaty of Versailles
1919	Treaty of St Germain (with Austria)
1919	Treaty of Neuilly (with Bulgaria)
1920	Treaty of Trianon (with Hungary)
1920	Polish occupation of Vilna
1921	Partition of Upper Silesia
1921	Aaland Islands Dispute
1921	Yugoslavian invasion of Albania
1922	League of Nations responds to Turkish refugee crisis
1923	Treaty of Lausanne
1923	Italian occupation of Corfu
1924	Dawes Plan
1925	Greek invasion of Bulgaria
1925	Locarno Treaties
1926	Germany joins the League of Nations

1928	Kellogg Briand Pact
1929	Great Depression
1931	Japanese invasion of Manchuria
1933	Japanese invasion of China
1934	Abyssinian border dispute with Italy
1935	The Saar becomes part of Germany
1935	Stresa Front
1935	Italy invades Abyssinia
1935	Hoare Laval Pact
1936	Remilitarisation of Rhineland
1936	Spanish Civil War begins
1937	Bombing of Guernica during the Spanish Civil War
1938	Anschluss
1938	Sudetenland crisis and Munich agreement
1939	Nazi-Soviet Pact
1939	German invasion of Poland
1939	Britain and France declare war on Germany

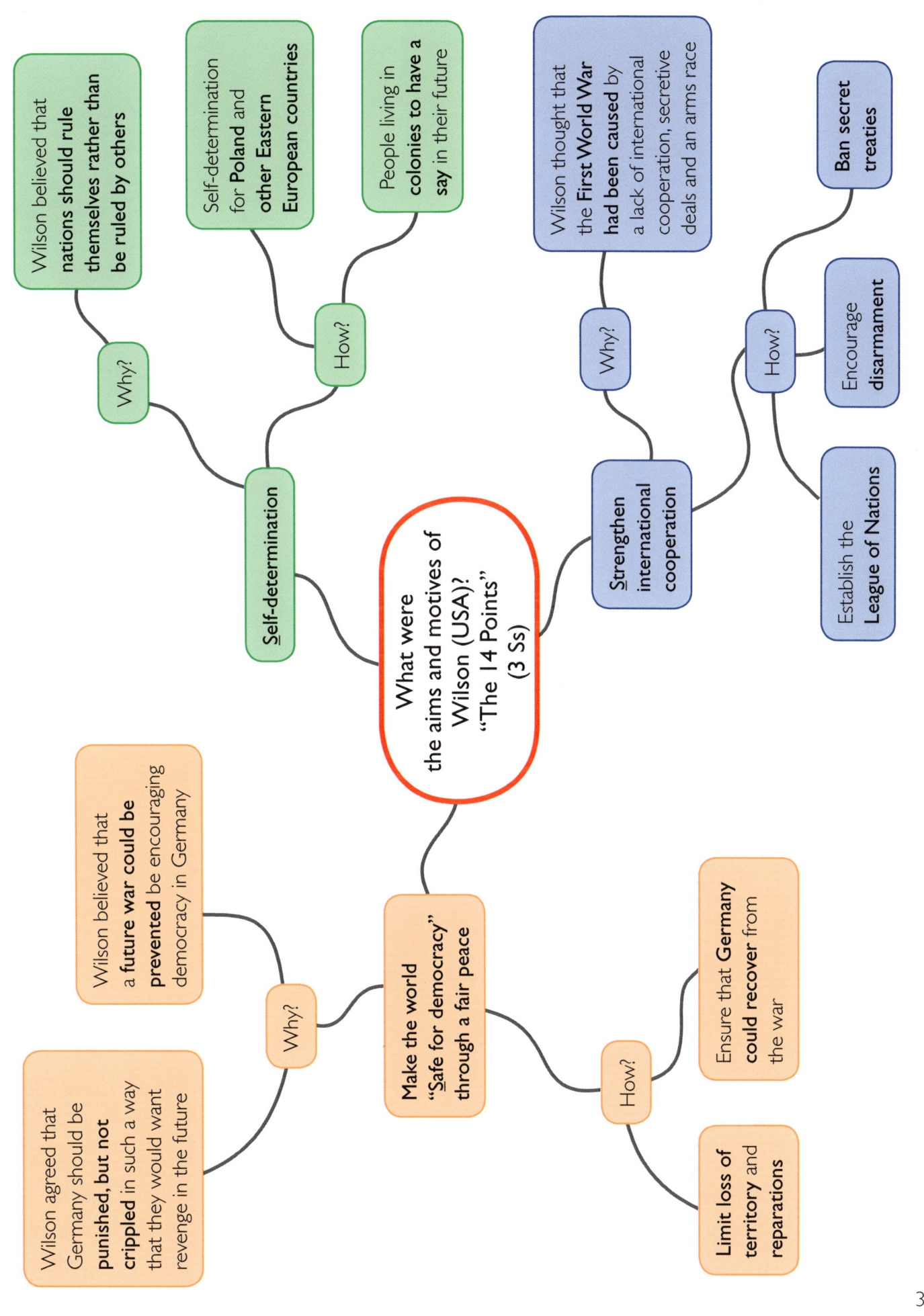

What were the aims and motives of Wilson (USA)? "The 14 Points" (3 Ss)

Self-determination

Why?
- Wilson believed that nations should rule themselves rather than be ruled by others

How?
- Self-determination for Poland and other Eastern European countries
- People living in colonies to have a say in their future

Strengthen international cooperation

Why?
- Wilson thought that the First World War had been caused by a lack of international cooperation, secretive deals and an arms race

How?
- Ban secret treaties
- Encourage disarmament
- Establish the League of Nations

Make the world "Safe for democracy" through a fair peace

Why?
- Wilson believed that a future war could be prevented be encouraging democracy in Germany
- Wilson agreed that Germany should be punished, but not crippled in such a way that they would want revenge in the future

How?
- Ensure that Germany could recover from the war
- Limit loss of territory and reparations

3

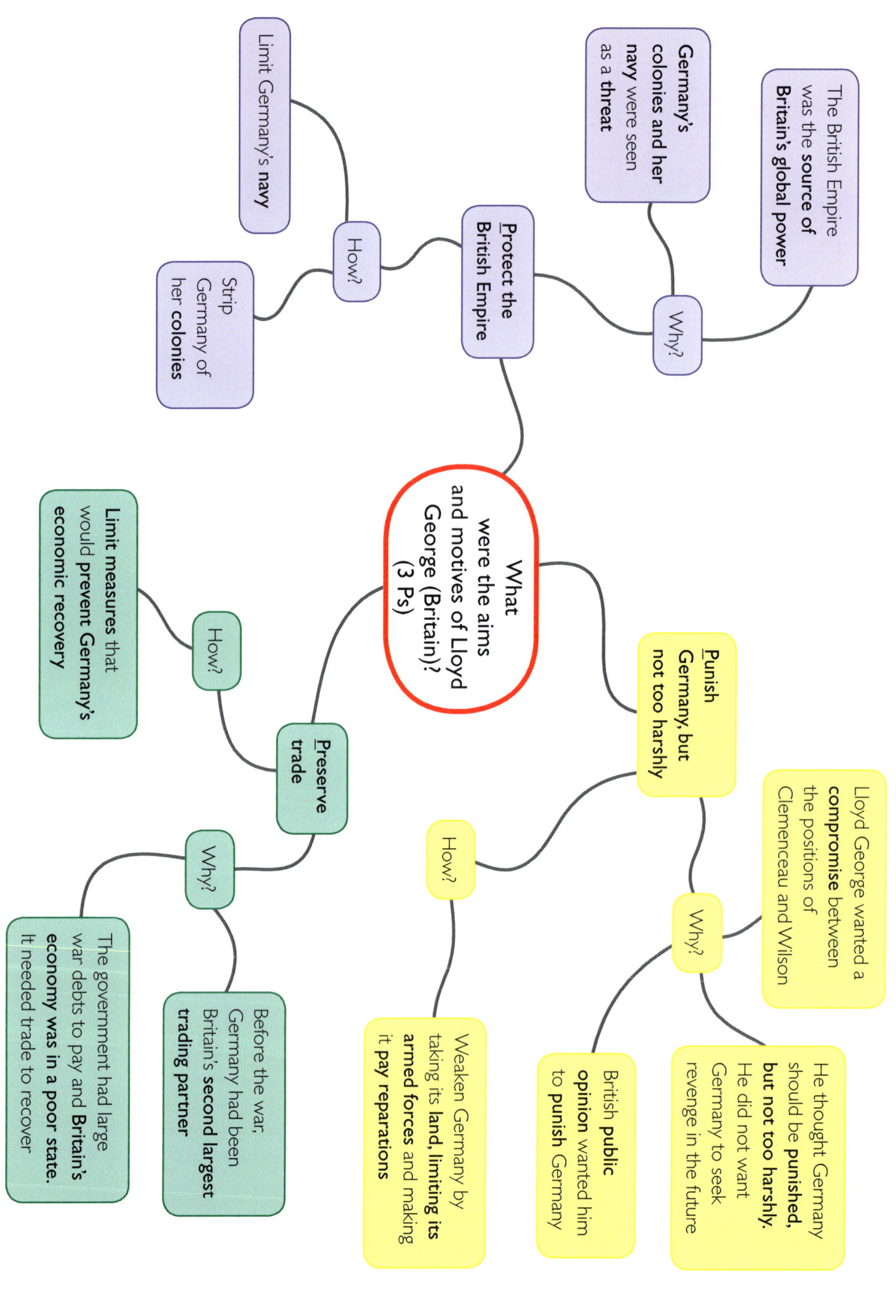

What were the aims and motives of Lloyd George (Britain)? (3 Ps)

Protect the British Empire

Why?
- The British Empire was the source of **Britain's global power**
- **Germany's colonies and her navy** were seen as a **threat**

How?
- Limit Germany's **navy**
- Strip Germany of her **colonies**

Preserve trade

How?
- **Limit measures** that would **prevent Germany's economic recovery**

Why?
- Before the war, Germany had been Britain's **second largest trading partner**
- The government had large war debts to pay and **Britain's economy was in a poor state.** It needed trade to recover

Punish Germany, but not too harshly

How?
- Weaken Germany by taking its **land, limiting its armed forces** and making it **pay reparations**

Why?
- British **public opinion** wanted him to **punish Germany**
- He thought Germany should be **punished, but not too harshly.** He did not want Germany to seek revenge in the future
- Lloyd George wanted a **compromise** between the positions of Clemenceau and Wilson

4

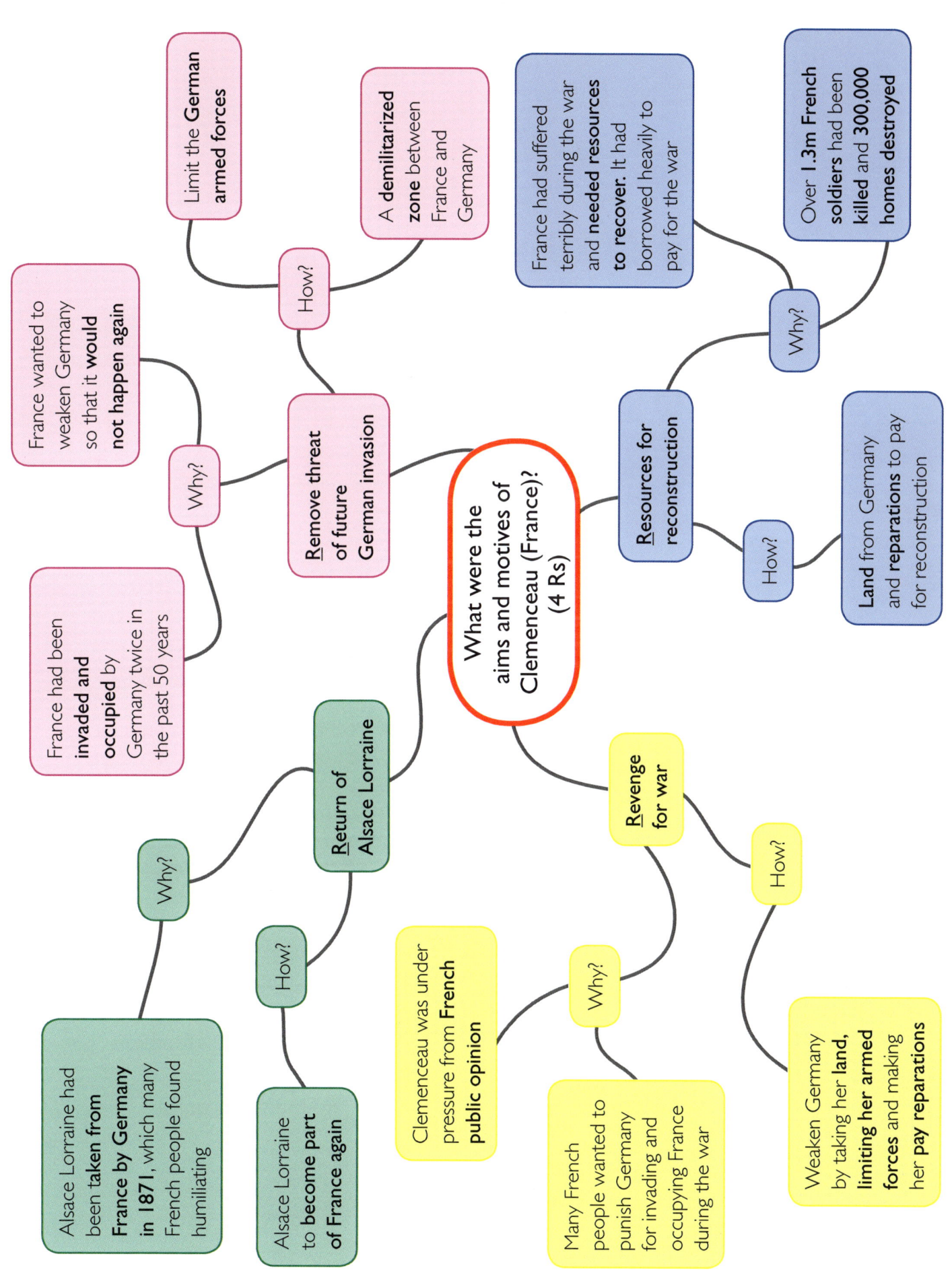

What were the aims and motives of Clemenceau (France)? (4 Rs)

Remove threat of future German invasion

How?
- Limit the German armed forces
- A demilitarized zone between France and Germany

Why?
- France wanted to weaken Germany so that it would not happen again
- France had been invaded and occupied by Germany twice in the past 50 years

Resources for reconstruction

Why?
- France had suffered terribly during the war and needed resources to recover. It had borrowed heavily to pay for the war
- Over 1.3m French soldiers had been killed and 300,000 homes destroyed

How?
- Land from Germany and reparations to pay for reconstruction

Return of Alsace Lorraine

Why?
- Alsace Lorraine had been taken from France by Germany in 1871, which many French people found humiliating

How?
- Alsace Lorraine to become part of France again

Revenge for war

Why?
- Clemenceau was under pressure from French public opinion
- Many French people wanted to punish Germany for invading and occupying France during the war

How?
- Weaken Germany by taking her land, limiting her armed forces and making her pay reparations

5

What were the terms of the Versailles Treaty?

War Guilt — Germany had to **accept blame** for the damage caused by the war

Armed forces
- **Conscription** was prohibited
- **Army** was limited to **100,000 men**
- **Navy** was limited to **15,000 men and 6 battleships**
- No **air force, armoured vehicles** or **submarines**
- **Rhineland** was demilitarized

Reparations — Germany had to pay reparations set at **£6,600 million**

Germany lost land
- Germany lost all her **colonies**. They were run by Britain and France as League of Nations mandates
- **Anschluss** (uniting with Austria) was prohibited
- **Lithuania, Latvia** and **Estonia** became independent countries (Germany had taken these territories from Russia in 1918)
- The **Rhineland** became a demilitarized zone
- **West Prussia, Posen** and **Upper Silesia** became part of **Poland**
- **Alsace Lorraine** was returned to **France**
- **North Schleswig** became part of Denmark
- **Danzig** was run by the League of Nations
- **Saar** region run by League of Nations for 15 years before plebiscite would decide its future

League of Nations — The League of Nations established

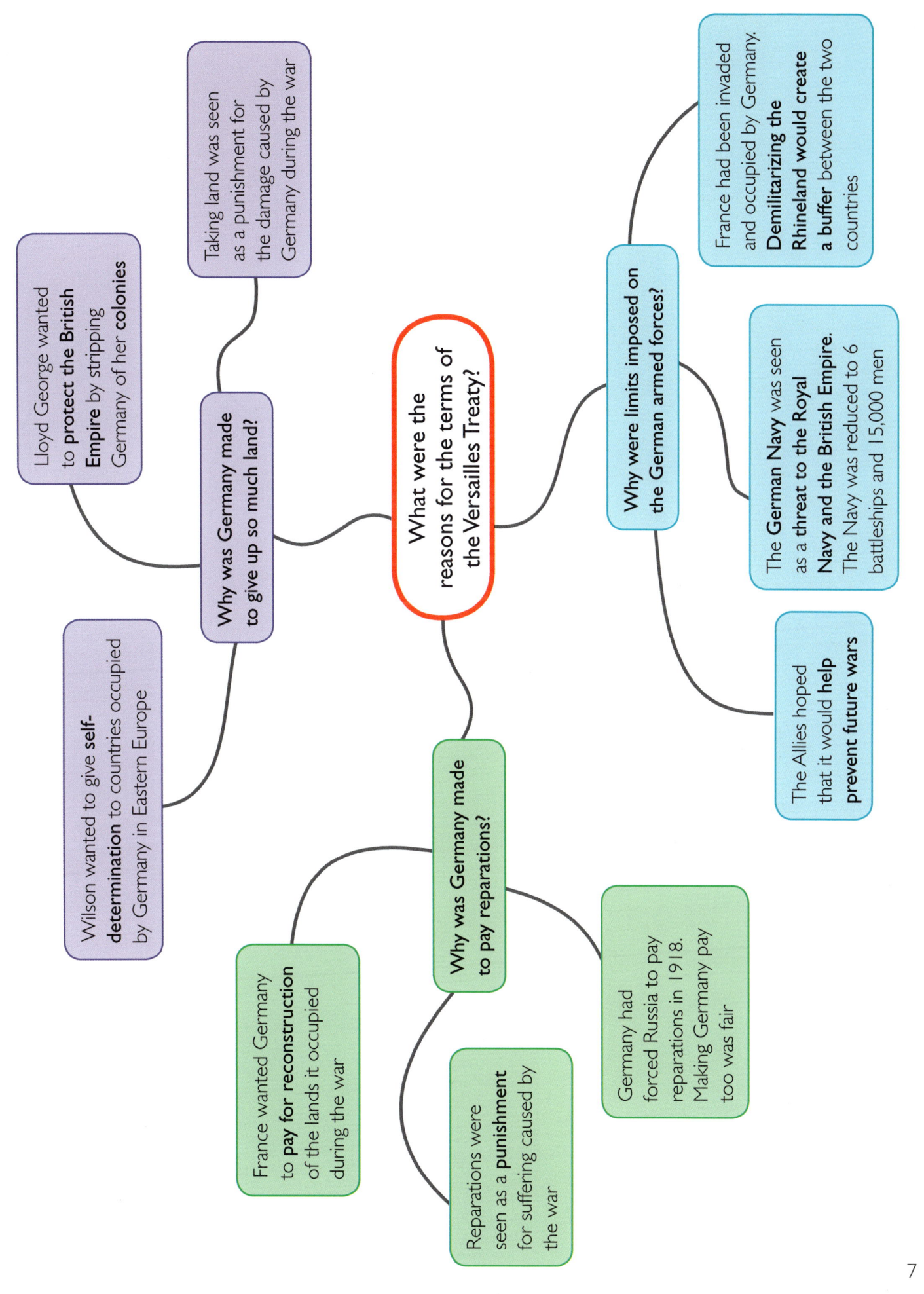

What were the reasons for the terms of the Versailles Treaty?

Why was Germany made to give up so much land?

Taking land was seen as a punishment for the damage caused by Germany during the war

Lloyd George wanted to **protect the British Empire** by stripping Germany of her **colonies**

Wilson wanted to give **self-determination** to countries occupied by Germany in Eastern Europe

Why were limits imposed on the German armed forces?

France had been invaded and occupied by Germany. **Demilitarizing the Rhineland** would create **a buffer** between the two countries

The German Navy was seen as a threat to the Royal Navy and the British Empire. The Navy was reduced to 6 battleships and 15,000 men

The Allies hoped that it would help **prevent future wars**

Why was Germany made to pay reparations?

France wanted Germany **to pay for reconstruction** of the lands it occupied during the war

Reparations were seen as a **punishment** for suffering caused by the war

Germany had forced Russia to pay reparations in 1918. Making Germany pay too was fair

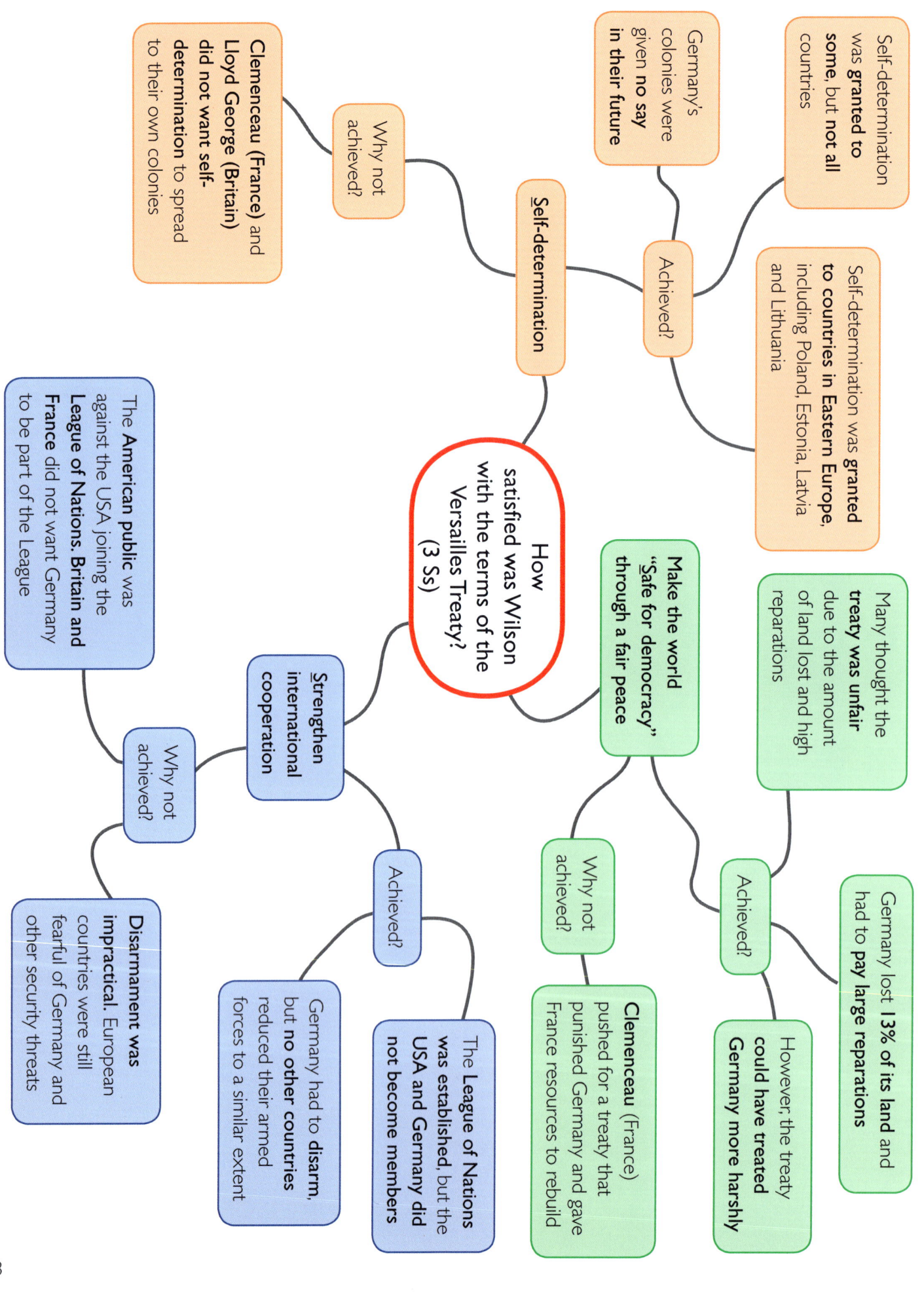

How satisfied was Wilson with the terms of the Versailles Treaty? (3 Ss)

Self-determination

Self-determination was **granted to some, but not all** countries

Germany's colonies were given **no say in their future**

Self-determination was **granted to countries in Eastern Europe**, including Poland, Estonia, Latvia and Lithuania

Achieved?

Why not achieved?

Clemenceau (France) and Lloyd George (Britain) **did not want self-determination** to spread to their own colonies

Make the world "Safe for democracy" through a fair peace

Many thought the **treaty was unfair** due to the amount of land lost and high reparations

Germany lost **13% of its land** and had to **pay large reparations**

Achieved?

However, the treaty **could have treated Germany more harshly**

Why not achieved?

Clemenceau (France) pushed for a treaty that punished Germany and gave France resources to rebuild

Strengthen international cooperation

Achieved?

The **League of Nations** was established, but the **USA and Germany did not become members**

Germany had to **disarm**, but **no other countries** reduced their armed forces to a similar extent

Why not achieved?

The **American public** was against the USA joining the **League of Nations. Britain and France** did not want Germany to be part of the League

Disarmament was impractical. European countries were still fearful of Germany and other security threats

8

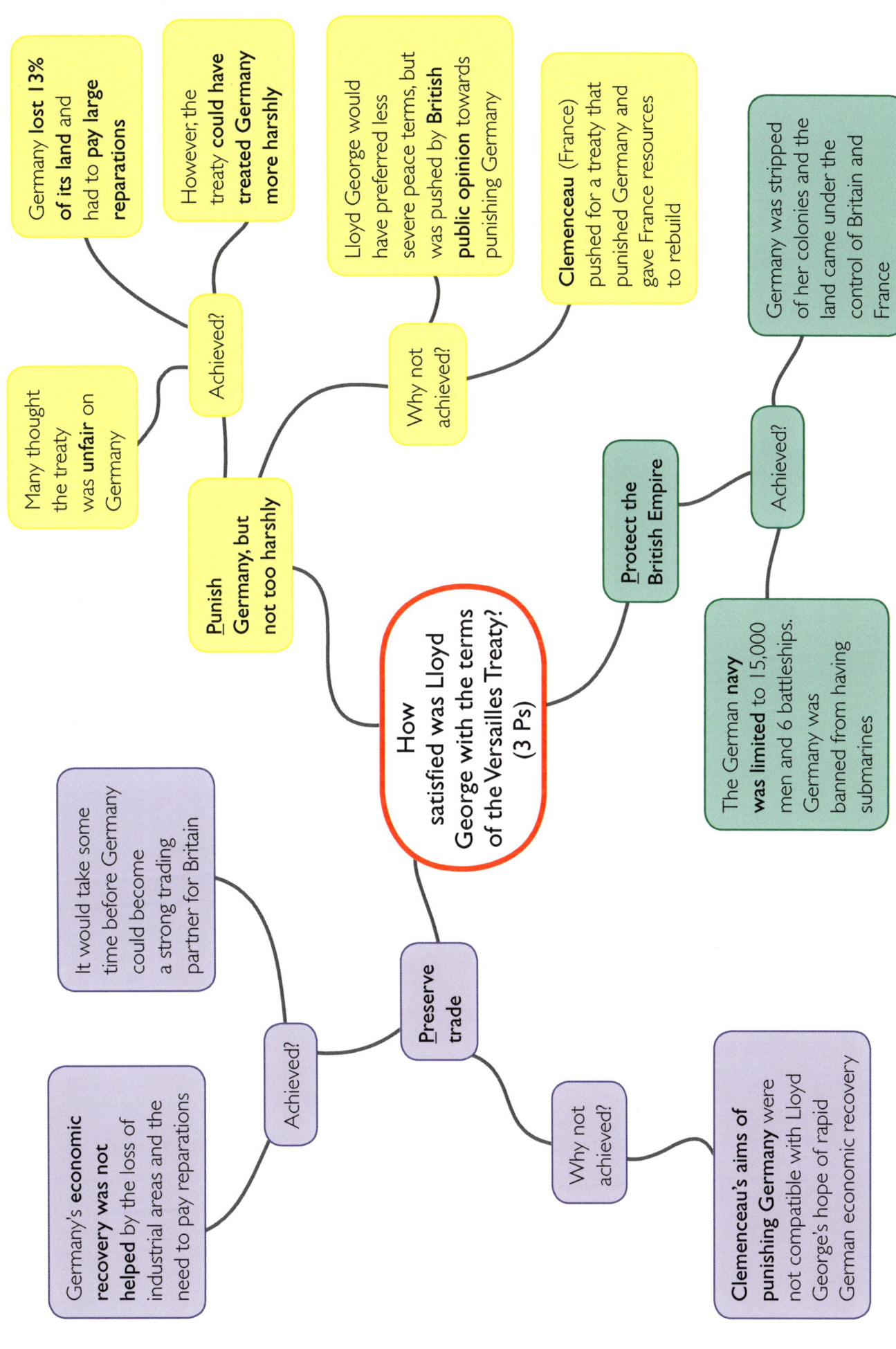

Germany lost 13% **of its land** and had to **pay large reparations**

However, the treaty **could have treated Germany more harshly**

Lloyd George would have preferred less severe peace terms, but was pushed by **British public opinion** towards punishing Germany

Clemenceau (France) pushed for a treaty that punished Germany and gave France resources to rebuild

Germany was stripped of her colonies and the land came under the control of Britain and France

Many thought the treaty was **unfair** on Germany

Achieved?

Why not achieved?

Protect the **B**ritish **E**mpire

Achieved?

Punish Germany, but not too harshly

How satisfied was Lloyd George with the terms of the Versailles Treaty? (3 Ps)

The German **navy was limited** to 15,000 men and 6 battleships. Germany was banned from having submarines

It would take some time before Germany could become a strong trading partner for Britain

Germany's **economic recovery was not helped** by the loss of industrial areas and the need to pay reparations

Achieved?

Preserve trade

Why not achieved?

Clemenceau's aims of punishing Germany were not compatible with Lloyd George's hope of rapid German economic recovery

9

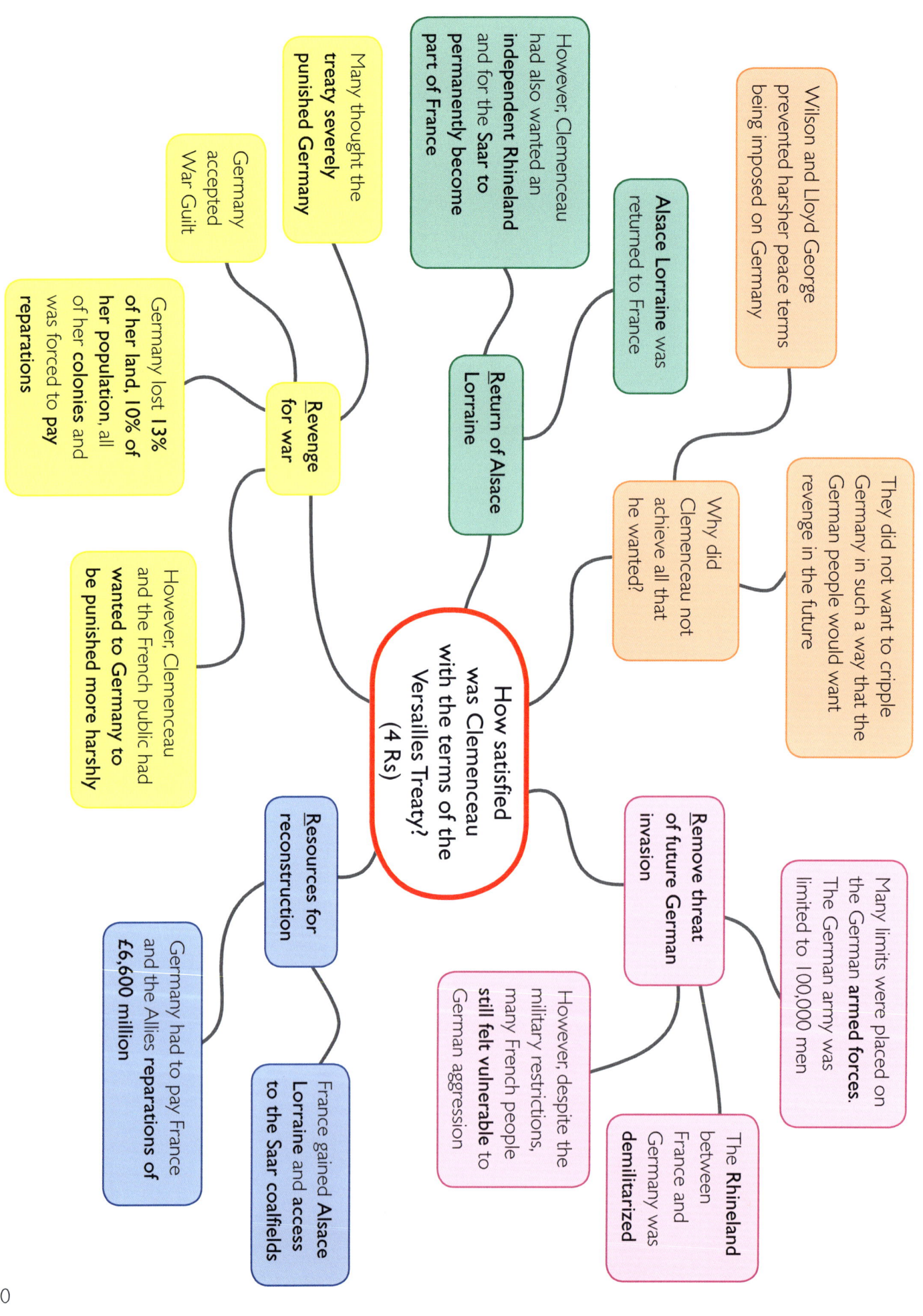

How satisfied was Clemenceau with the terms of the Versailles Treaty? (4 Rs)

Revenge for war

Many thought the **treaty severely punished Germany**

Germany accepted War Guilt

Germany lost **13% of her land, 10% of her population**, all of her colonies and was forced to **pay reparations**

However, Clemenceau and the French public had **wanted to Germany to be punished more harshly**

Return of Alsace Lorraine

Alsace Lorraine was returned to France

However, Clemenceau had also wanted an **independent Rhineland** and for the **Saar to permanently become part of France**

Why did Clemenceau not achieve all that he wanted?

Wilson and Lloyd George prevented harsher peace terms being imposed on Germany

They did not want to cripple Germany in such a way that the German people would want revenge in the future

Remove threat of future German invasion

Many limits were placed on the German **armed forces.** The German army was limited to 100,000 men

The **Rhineland** between France and Germany was **demilitarized**

However, despite the military restrictions, many French people **still felt vulnerable to** German aggression

Resources for reconstruction

Germany had to pay France and the Allies **reparations of £6,600 million**

France gained **Alsace Lorraine and access to the Saar coalfields**

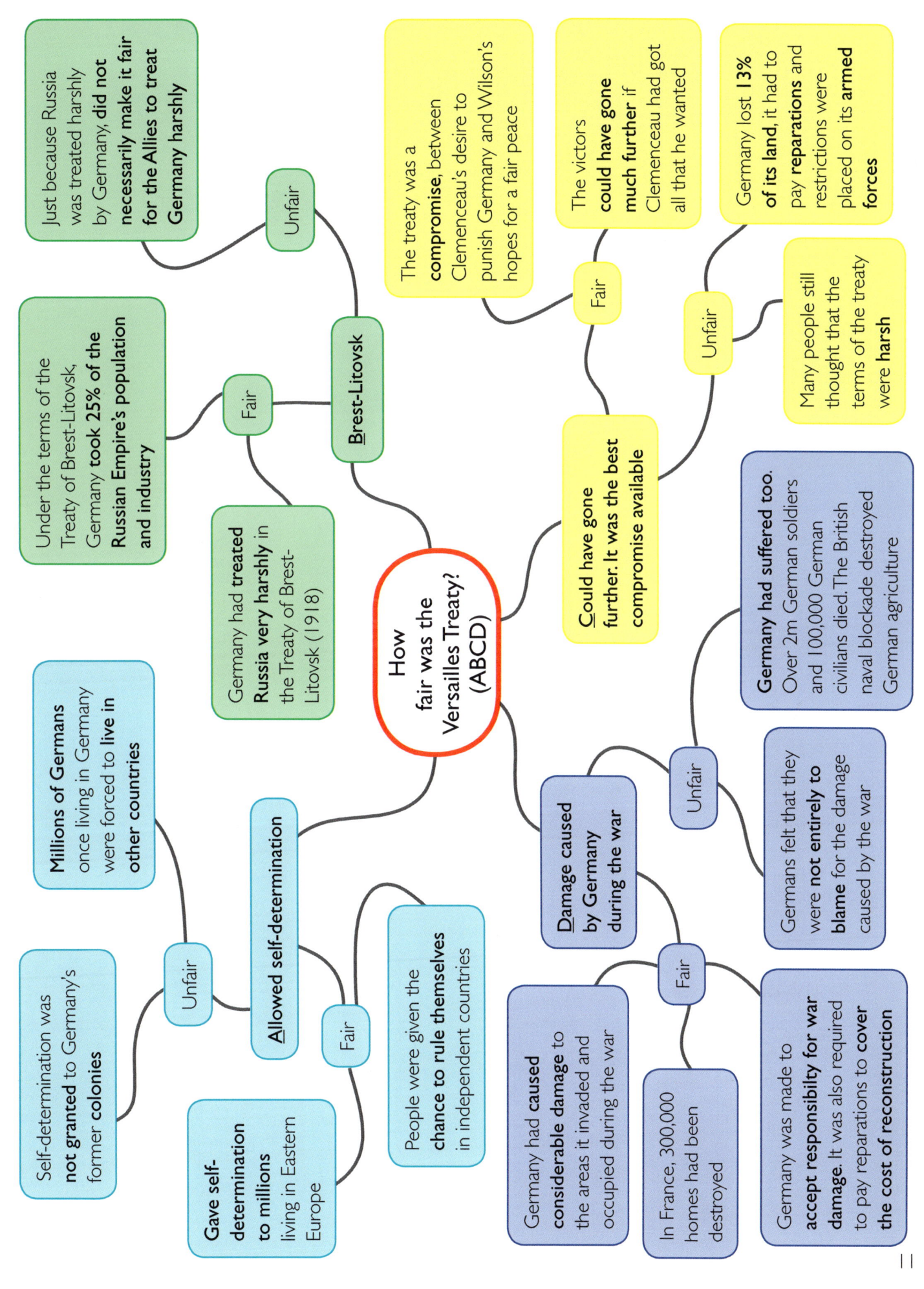

How fair was the Versailles Treaty? (ABCD)

Brest-Litovsk

Fair — Under the terms of the Treaty of Brest-Litovsk, Germany took **25% of the Russian Empire's population and industry**

Fair — Germany had treated **Russia very harshly** in the Treaty of Brest-Litovsk (1918)

Unfair — Just because Russia was treated harshly by Germany, **did not necessarily make it fair for the Allies to treat Germany harshly**

Fair — The treaty was a **compromise**, between Clemenceau's desire to punish Germany and Wilson's hopes for a fair peace

Fair — The victors **could have gone much further** if Clemenceau had got all that he wanted

Fair — <u>C</u>ould have gone further. It was the best compromise available

Unfair — Germany lost **13% of its land**, it had to pay **reparations** and restrictions were placed on its **armed forces**

Unfair — Many people still thought that the terms of the treaty were **harsh**

Unfair — **Germany had suffered too.** Over 2m German soldiers and 100,000 German civilians died. The British naval blockade destroyed German agriculture

Damage caused by Germany during the war

Unfair — Germans felt that they were **not entirely to blame** for the damage caused by the war

Fair — Germany had caused **considerable damage** to the areas it invaded and occupied during the war

Fair — In France, 300,000 homes had been destroyed

Fair — Germany was made to **accept responsibility for war damage.** It was also required to pay reparations to **cover the cost of reconstruction**

Allowed self-determination

Unfair — **Millions of Germans** once living in Germany were forced to live in other countries

Unfair — Self-determination was **not granted** to Germany's former colonies

Fair — **Gave self-determination to millions** living in Eastern Europe

Fair — People were given the **chance to rule themselves** in independent countries

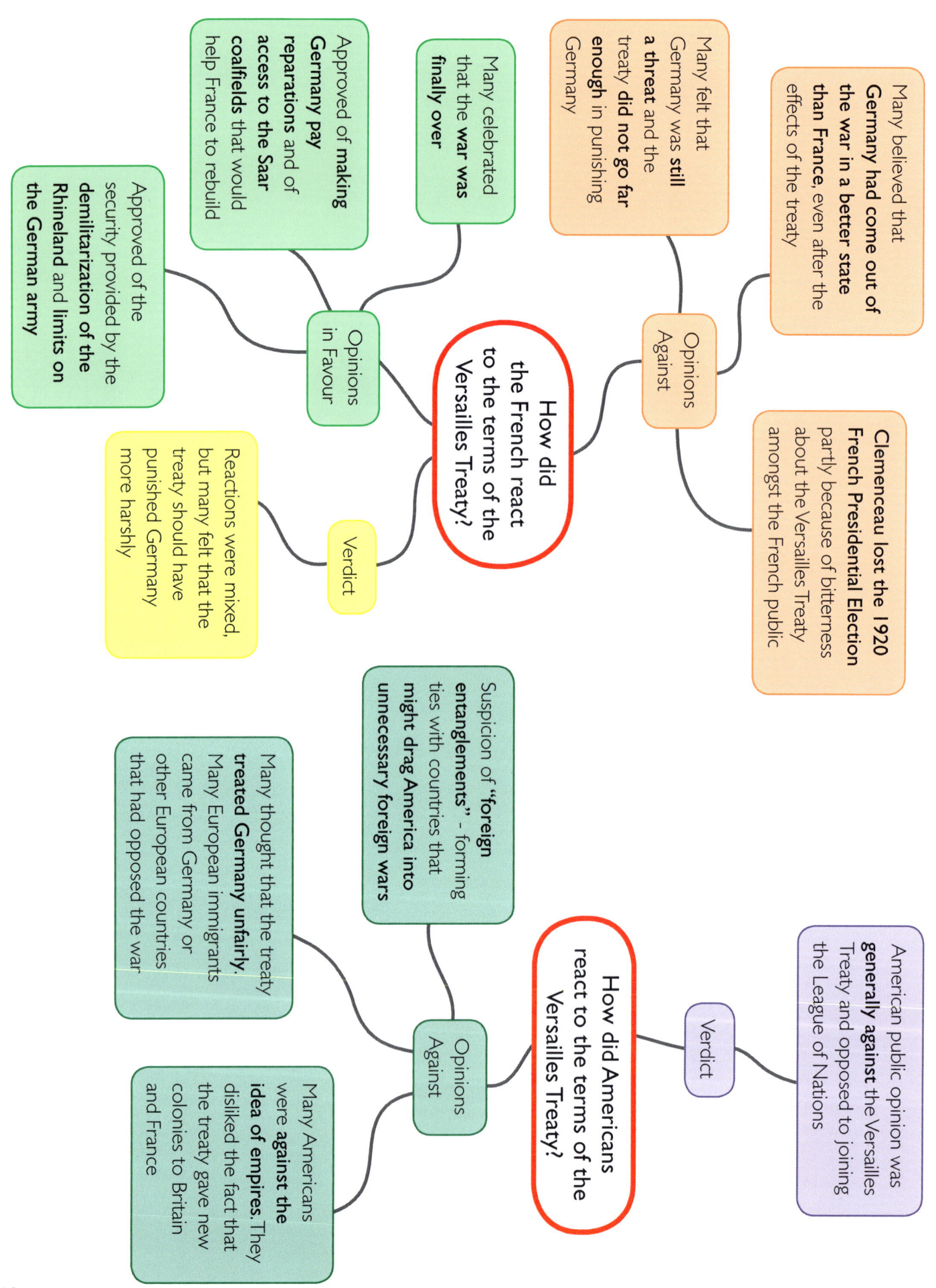

How did the French react to the terms of the Versailles Treaty?

Opinions in Favour

- Many celebrated that the **war was finally over**

- Approved of making **Germany pay reparations** and of **access to the Saar coalfields** that would help France to rebuild

- Approved of the security provided by the **demilitarization of the Rhineland and limits on the German army**

Verdict

- Reactions were mixed, but many felt that the treaty should have punished Germany more harshly

Opinions Against

- Many felt that Germany was **still a threat** and the treaty **did not go far enough** in punishing Germany

- Many believed that **Germany had come out of the war in a better state than France**, even after the effects of the treaty

- **Clemenceau lost the 1920 French Presidential Election** partly because of bitterness about the Versailles Treaty amongst the French public

How did Americans react to the terms of the Versailles Treaty?

Opinions Against

- Suspicion of **"foreign entanglements"** - forming ties with countries that **might drag America into unnecessary foreign wars**

- Many thought that the treaty **treated Germany unfairly.** Many European immigrants came from Germany or other European countries that had opposed the war

- Many Americans were **against the idea of empires.** They disliked the fact that the treaty gave new colonies to Britain and France

Verdict

- American public opinion was **generally against** the Versailles Treaty and opposed to joining the League of Nations

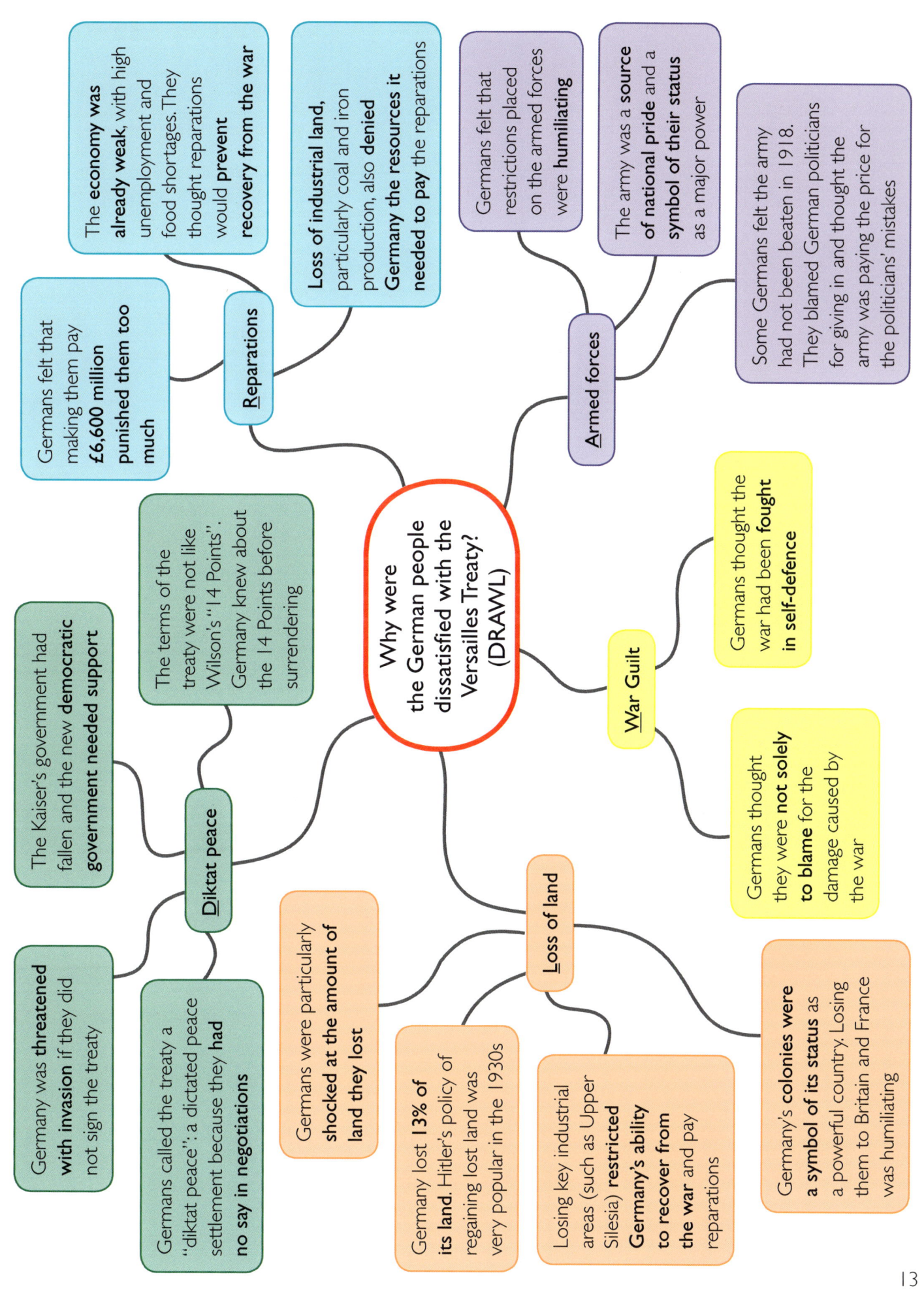

Why were the German people dissatisfied with the Versailles Treaty? (DRAWL)

Reparations

The economy was **already weak**, with high unemployment and food shortages. They thought reparations would **prevent recovery from the war**

Germans felt that making them pay **£6,600 million punished them too much**

Loss of industrial land, particularly coal and iron production, also **denied Germany the resources it needed to pay** the reparations

Armed forces

Germans felt that restrictions placed on the armed forces were **humiliating**

The army was a **source of national pride** and a **symbol of their status** as a major power

Some Germans felt the army had not been beaten in 1918. They blamed German politicians for giving in and thought the army was paying the price for the politicians' mistakes

Diktat peace

The Kaiser's government had fallen and the new **democratic government needed support**

The terms of the treaty were not like Wilson's "14 Points". Germany knew about the 14 Points before surrendering

Germany was **threatened with invasion** if they did not sign the treaty

Germans called the treaty a "diktat peace"; a dictated peace settlement because they had **no say in negotiations**

War Guilt

Germans thought the war had been **fought in self-defence**

Germans thought they were **not solely to blame** for the damage caused by the war

Loss of land

Germans were particularly **shocked at the amount of land they lost**

Germany lost **13% of its land.** Hitler's policy of regaining lost land was very popular in the 1930s

Losing key industrial areas (such as Upper Silesia) **restricted Germany's ability to recover from the war** and pay reparations

Germany's colonies were **a symbol of its status** as a powerful country. Losing them to Britain and France was humiliating

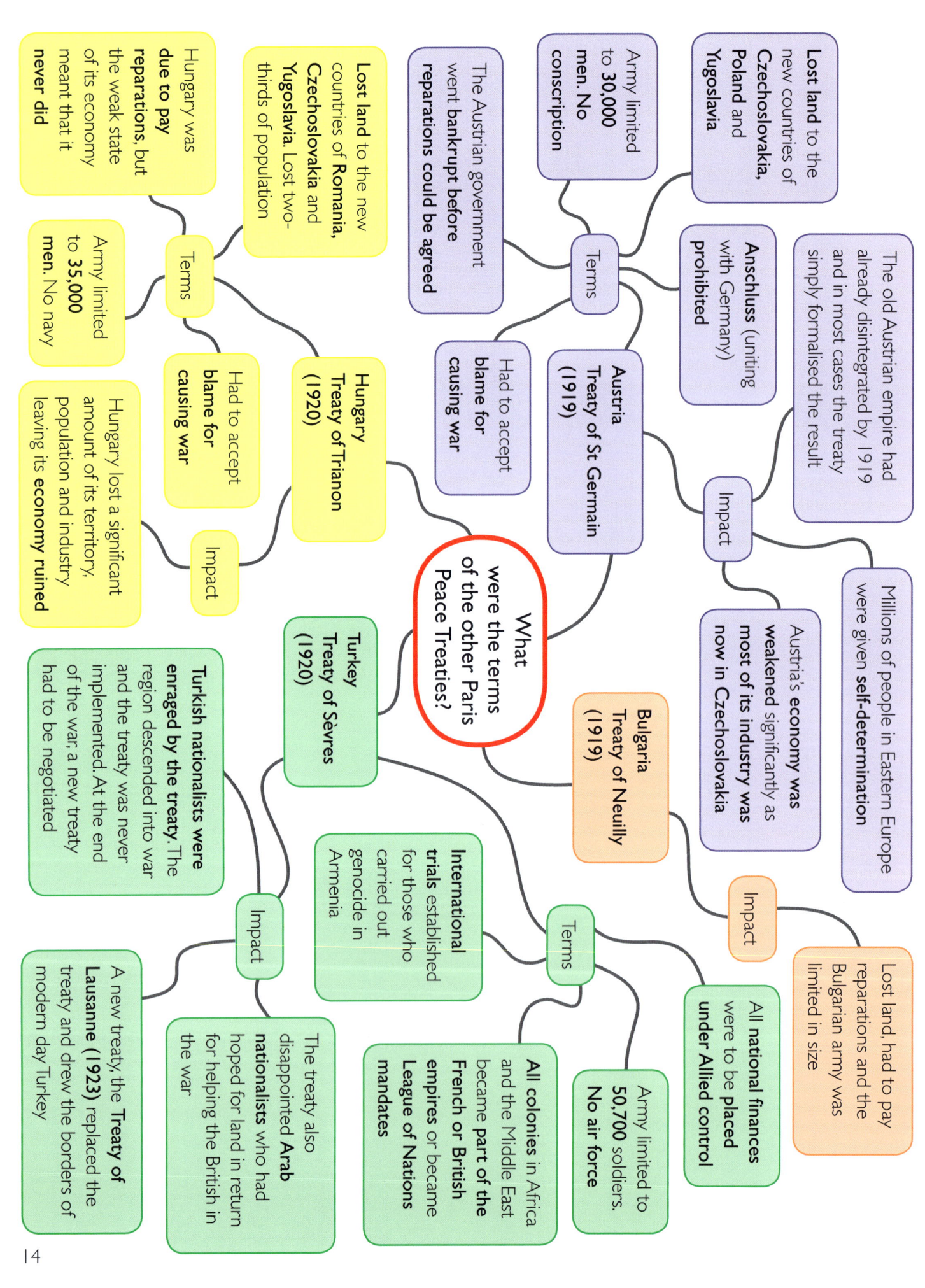

What were the terms of the other Paris Peace Treaties?

Austria Treaty of St Germain (1919)

Terms
- Lost land to the new countries of **Czechoslovakia, Poland and Yugoslavia**
- Army limited to 30,000 men. No conscription
- The Austrian government went **bankrupt before reparations could be agreed**
- **Anschluss** (uniting with Germany) **prohibited**
- Had to accept **blame for causing war**

Impact
- The old Austrian empire had already disintegrated by 1919 and in most cases the treaty simply formalised the result
- Millions of people in Eastern Europe were given **self-determination**
- Austria's economy was **weakened** significantly as most of its industry was now in Czechoslovakia

Hungary Treaty of Trianon (1920)

Terms
- Hungary was **due to pay reparations**, but the weak state of its economy meant that it **never did**
- Lost land to the new countries of **Romania, Czechoslovakia and Yugoslavia.** Lost two-thirds of population
- Army limited to **35,000 men.** No navy
- Had to accept **blame for causing war**

Impact
- Hungary lost a significant amount of its territory, population and industry leaving its **economy ruined**

Turkey Treaty of Sèvres (1920)

Terms
- International **trials** established for those who carried out genocide in Armenia
- All colonies in Africa and the Middle East became **part of the French or British empires** or became **League of Nations mandates**
- Army limited to **50,700 soldiers. No air force**

Impact
- Turkish nationalists were **enraged by the treaty.** The region descended into war and the treaty was never implemented. At the end of the war, a new treaty had to be negotiated
- The treaty also disappointed **Arab nationalists** who had hoped for land in return for helping the British in the war
- A new treaty, the **Treaty of Lausanne (1923)** replaced the treaty and drew the borders of modern day Turkey

Bulgaria Treaty of Neuilly (1919)

Terms
- All **national finances** were to be placed **under Allied control**

Impact
- Lost land, had to pay reparations and the Bulgarian army was limited in size

14

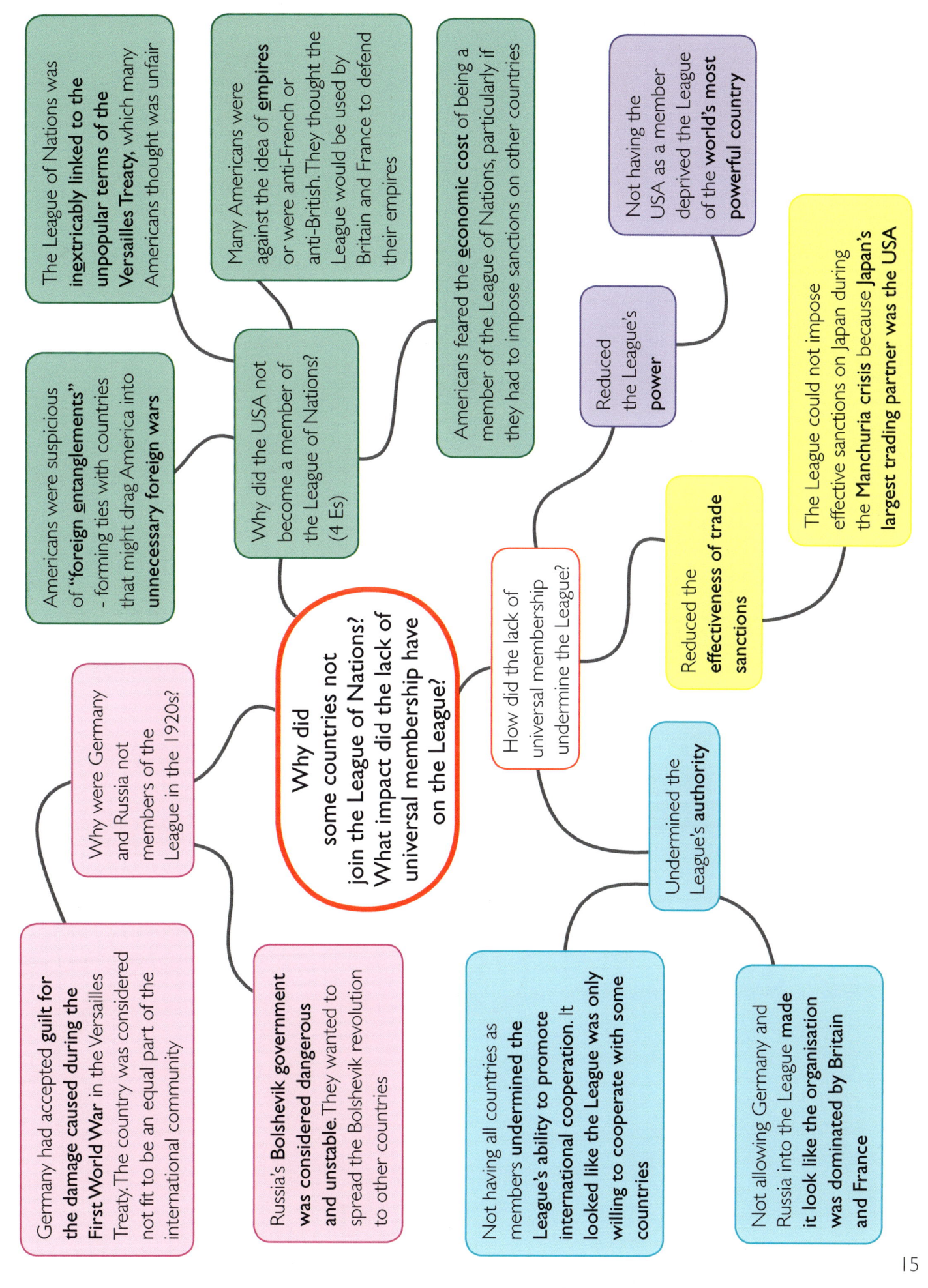

Why did some countries not join the League of Nations? What impact did the lack of universal membership have on the League?

The League of Nations was **inextricably linked to the unpopular terms of the Versailles Treaty,** which many Americans thought was unfair

Americans were suspicious of **"foreign entanglements"** – forming ties with countries that might drag America into **unnecessary foreign wars**

Many Americans were against the idea of **empires** or were anti-French or anti-British. They thought the League would be used by Britain and France to defend their empires

Why did the USA not become a member of the League of Nations? (4 Es)

Americans feared the **economic cost** of being a member of the League of Nations, particularly if they had to impose sanctions on other countries

Not having the USA as a member deprived the League of the **world's most powerful country**

Reduced the League's **power**

The League could not impose effective sanctions on Japan during the **Manchuria crisis** because Japan's **largest trading partner was the USA**

Reduced the **effectiveness of trade sanctions**

How did the lack of universal membership undermine the League?

Undermined the League's **authority**

Why were Germany and Russia not members of the League in the 1920s?

Germany had accepted **guilt for the damage caused during the First World War** in the Versailles Treaty. The country was considered not fit to be an equal part of the international community

Russia's **Bolshevik government was considered dangerous and unstable.** They wanted to spread the Bolshevik revolution to other countries

Not having all countries as members **undermined the League's ability to promote international cooperation.** It looked like the League was only **willing to cooperate with some countries**

Not allowing Germany and Russia into the League made **it look like the organisation was dominated by Britain and France**

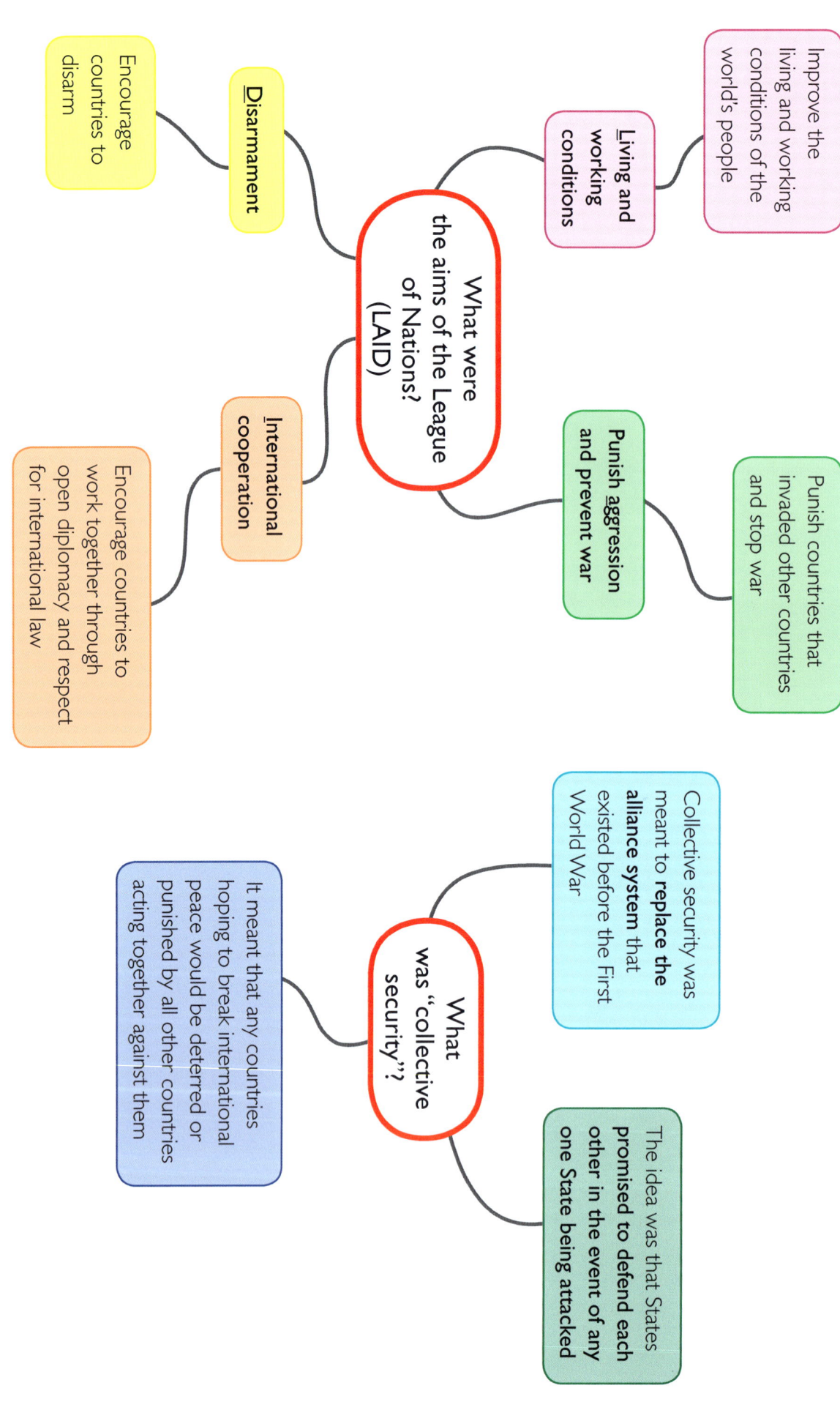

What were the aims of the League of Nations? (LAID)

Disarmament
- Encourage countries to disarm

Living and working conditions
- Improve the living and working conditions of the world's people

International cooperation
- Encourage countries to work together through open diplomacy and respect for international law

Punish aggression and prevent war
- Punish countries that invaded other countries and stop war

What was "collective security"?
- Collective security was meant to **replace the alliance system** that existed before the First World War
- It meant that any countries hoping to break international peace would be deterred or punished by all other countries acting together against them
- The idea was that States promised to defend each other in the event of any one State being attacked

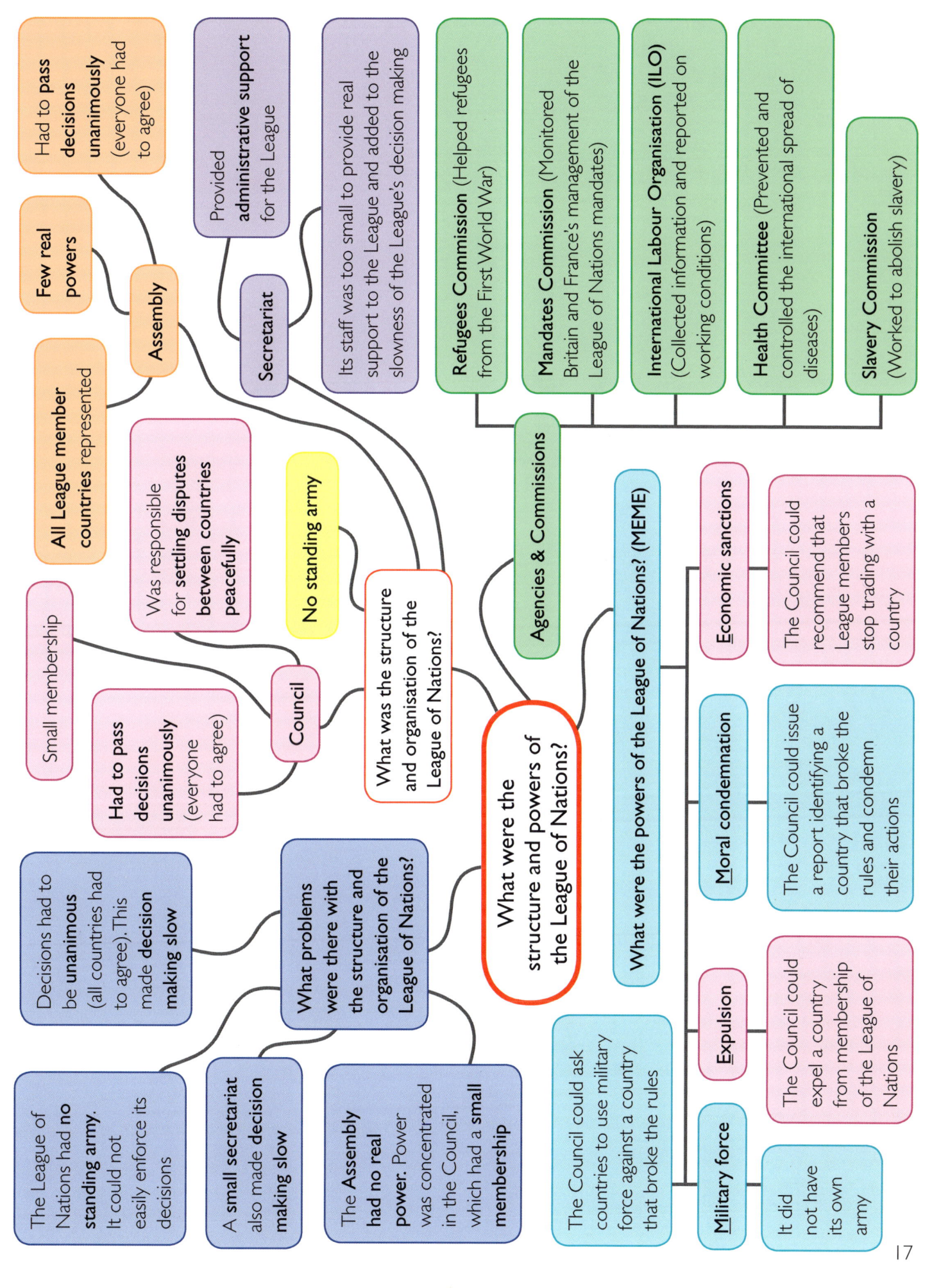

What were the structure and powers of the League of Nations?

What was the structure and organisation of League of Nations?

Assembly
- Had to pass decisions unanimously (everyone had to agree)
- Few real powers
- All League member countries represented

Secretariat
- Provided administrative support for the League
- Its staff was too small to provide real support to the League and added to the slowness of the League's decision making

Council
- Was responsible for settling disputes between countries peacefully
- Small membership
- Had to pass decisions unanimously (everyone had to agree)
- No standing army

Agencies & Commissions
- Refugees Commission (Helped refugees from the First World War)
- Mandates Commission (Monitored Britain and France's management of the League of Nations mandates)
- International Labour Organisation (ILO) (Collected information and reported on working conditions)
- Health Committee (Prevented and controlled the international spread of diseases)
- Slavery Commission (Worked to abolish slavery)

What problems were there with the structure and organisation of the League of Nations?
- Decisions had to be unanimous (all countries had to agree). This made decision making slow
- The League of Nations had no standing army. It could not easily enforce its decisions
- A small secretariat also made decision making slow
- The Assembly had no real power. Power was concentrated in the Council, which had a small membership

What were the powers of the League of Nations? (MEME)

Military force
- It did not have its own army
- The Council could ask countries to use military force against a country that broke the rules

Expulsion
- The Council could expel a country from membership of the League of Nations

Moral condemnation
- The Council could issue a report identifying a country that broke the rules and condemn their actions

Economic sanctions
- The Council could recommend that League members stop trading with a country

17

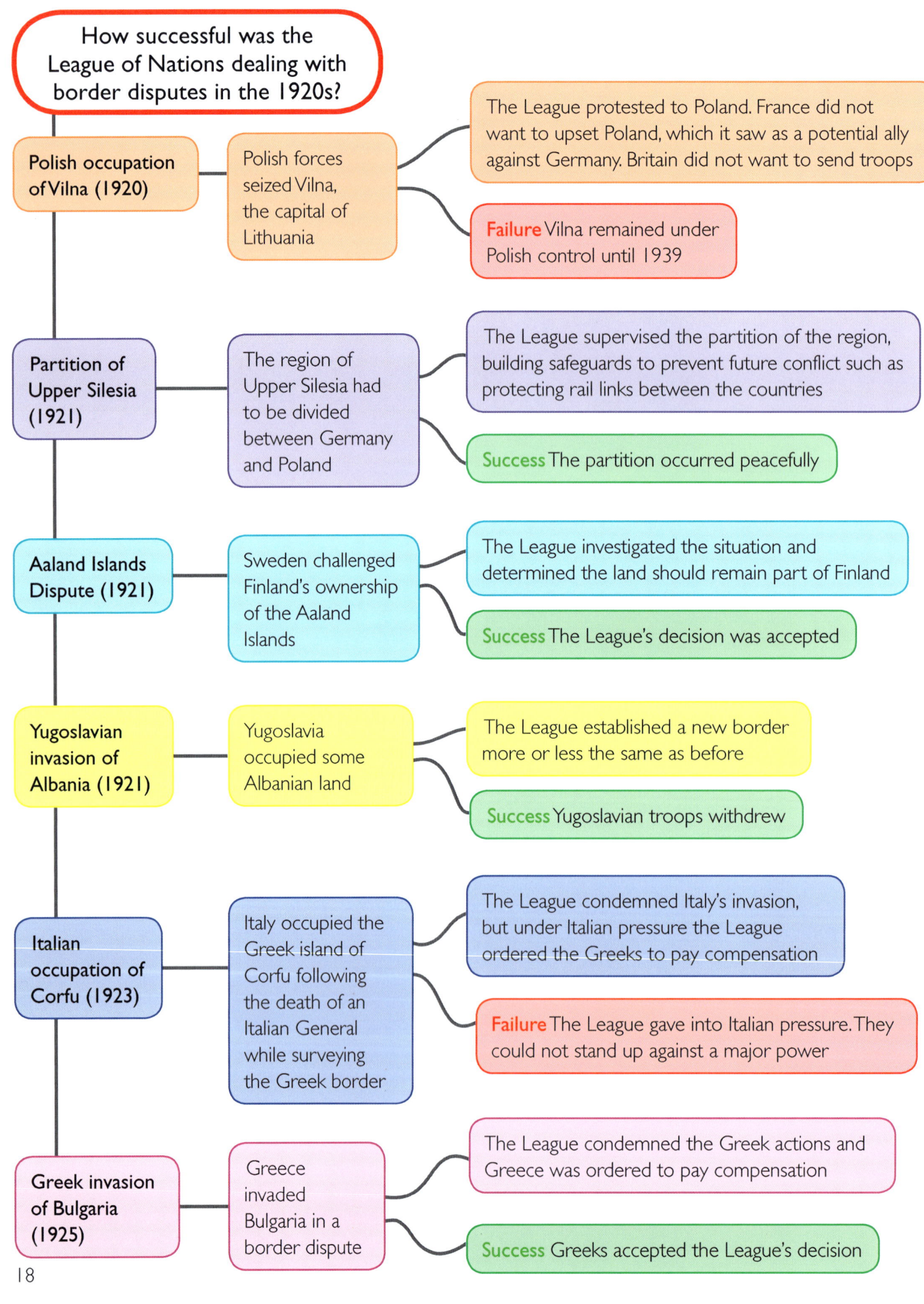

How successful was the League of Nations dealing with border disputes in the 1920s?

Polish occupation of Vilna (1920)

Polish forces seized Vilna, the capital of Lithuania

The League protested to Poland. France did not want to upset Poland, which it saw as a potential ally against Germany. Britain did not want to send troops

Failure Vilna remained under Polish control until 1939

Partition of Upper Silesia (1921)

The region of Upper Silesia had to be divided between Germany and Poland

The League supervised the partition of the region, building safeguards to prevent future conflict such as protecting rail links between the countries

Success The partition occurred peacefully

Aaland Islands Dispute (1921)

Sweden challenged Finland's ownership of the Aaland Islands

The League investigated the situation and determined the land should remain part of Finland

Success The League's decision was accepted

Yugoslavian invasion of Albania (1921)

Yugoslavia occupied some Albanian land

The League established a new border more or less the same as before

Success Yugoslavian troops withdrew

Italian occupation of Corfu (1923)

Italy occupied the Greek island of Corfu following the death of an Italian General while surveying the Greek border

The League condemned Italy's invasion, but under Italian pressure the League ordered the Greeks to pay compensation

Failure The League gave into Italian pressure. They could not stand up against a major power

Greek invasion of Bulgaria (1925)

Greece invaded Bulgaria in a border dispute

The League condemned the Greek actions and Greece was ordered to pay compensation

Success Greeks accepted the League's decision

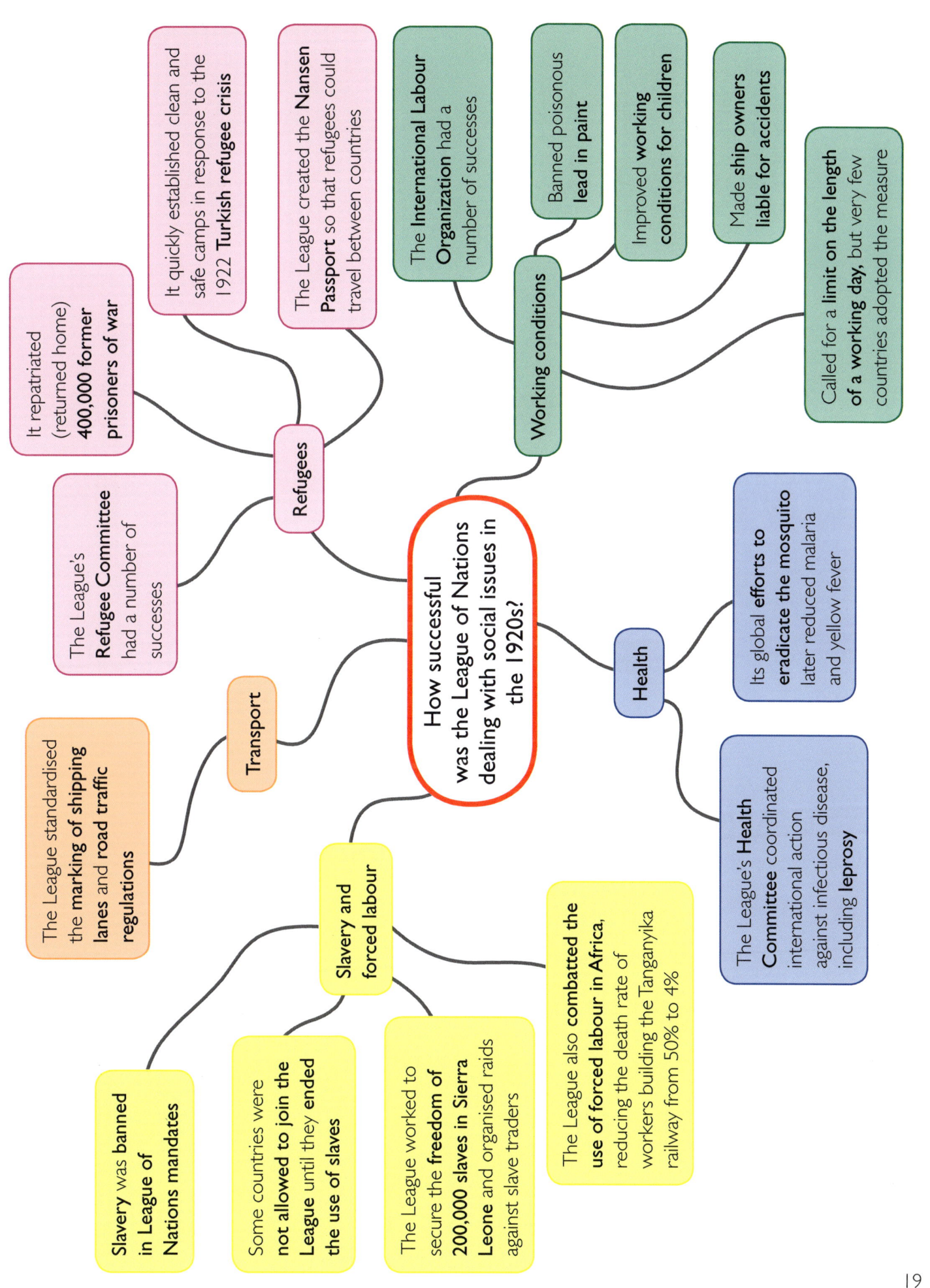

How successful was the League of Nations dealing with social issues in the 1920s?

Refugees

It repatriated (returned home) **400,000 former prisoners of war**

It quickly established clean and safe camps in response to the 1922 **Turkish refugee crisis**

The League created the **Nansen Passport** so that refugees could travel between countries

The League's **Refugee Committee** had a number of successes

Working conditions

The **International Labour Organization** had a number of successes

Banned poisonous **lead in paint**

Improved **working conditions for children**

Made **ship owners liable for accidents**

Called for a limit on the length **of a working day,** but very few countries adopted the measure

Health

Its global **efforts to eradicate the mosquito** later reduced malaria and yellow fever

The League's **Health Committee** coordinated international action against infectious disease, including **leprosy**

Transport

The League standardised the **marking of shipping lanes** and road traffic regulations

Slavery and forced labour

Slavery was banned **in League of Nations mandates**

Some countries were **not allowed to join the League until they ended the use of slaves**

The League worked to secure the **freedom of 200,000 slaves in Sierra Leone** and organised raids against slave traders

The League also **combatted the use of forced labour in Africa,** reducing the death rate of workers building the Tanganyika railway from 50% to 4%

19

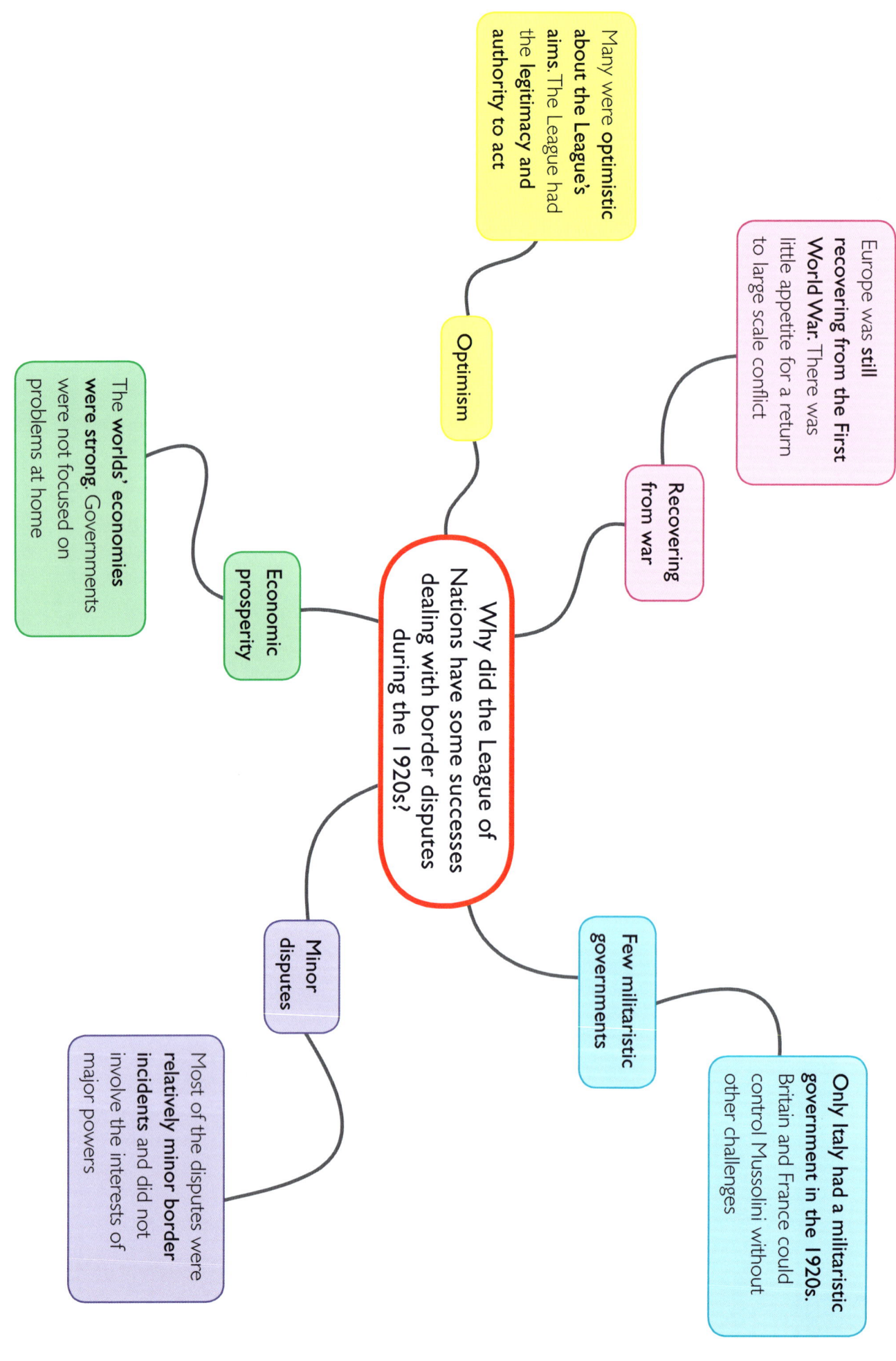

Why did the League of Nations have some successes dealing with border disputes during the 1920s?

Optimism
Many were **optimistic about the League's aims.** The League had the **legitimacy and authority to act**

Recovering from war
Europe was **still recovering from the First World War.** There was little appetite for a return to large scale conflict

Economic prosperity
The **worlds' economies were strong.** Governments were not focused on problems at home

Minor disputes
Most of the disputes were **relatively minor border incidents** and did not involve the interests of major powers

Few militaristic governments
Only Italy had a militaristic **government in the 1920s.** Britain and France could control Mussolini without other challenges

20

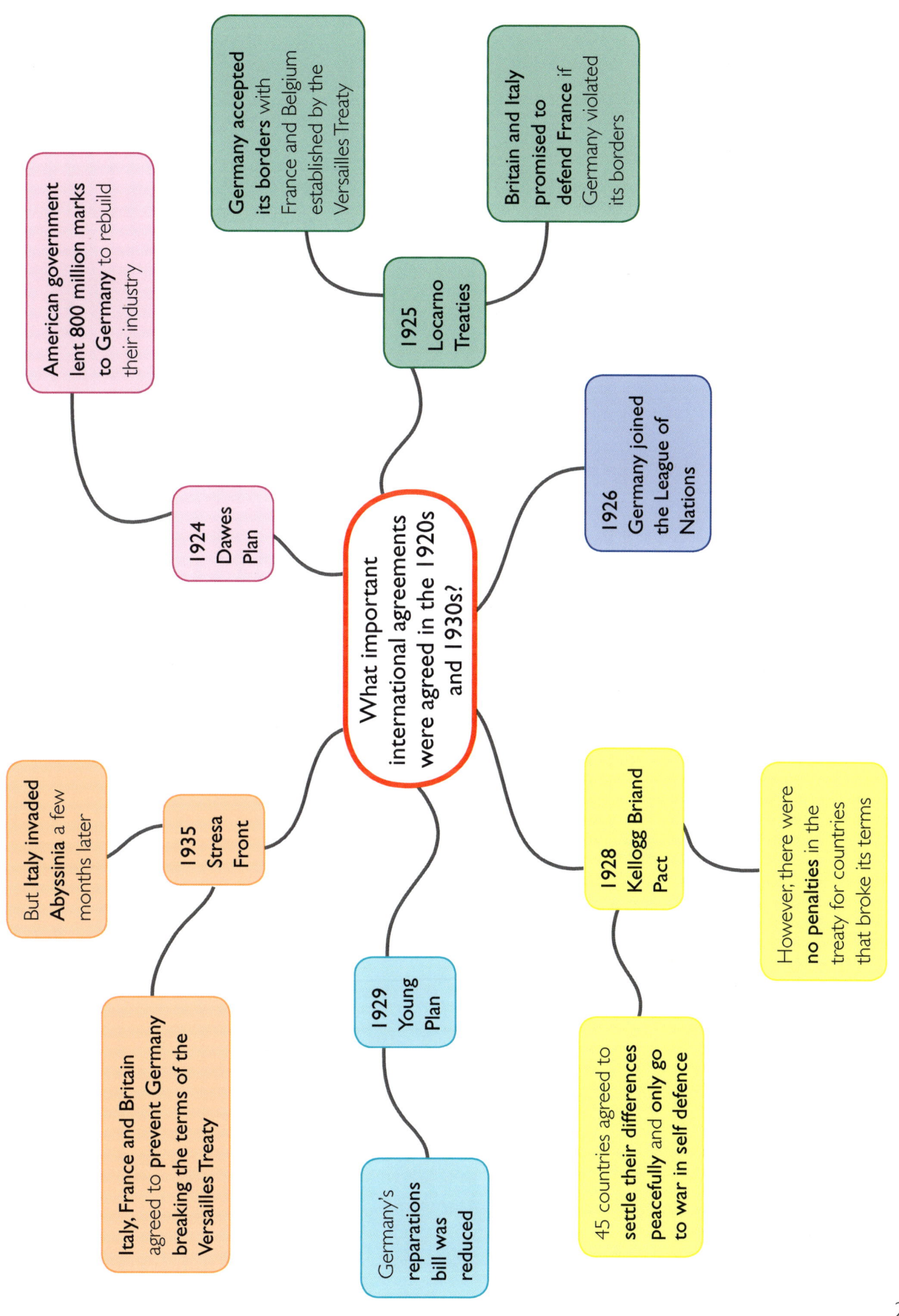

What important international agreements were agreed in the 1920s and 1930s?

1924 Dawes Plan
American government lent **800 million marks to Germany** to rebuild their industry

1925 Locarno Treaties
Germany accepted its borders with France and Belgium established by the Versailles Treaty

Britain and Italy **promised to defend France** if Germany violated its borders

1926 Germany joined the League of Nations

1928 Kellogg Briand Pact
45 countries agreed to **settle their differences peacefully** and only go to war in self defence

However, there were **no penalties** in the treaty for countries that broke its terms

1929 Young Plan
Germany's reparations bill was reduced

1935 Stresa Front
Italy, France and Britain agreed to prevent Germany breaking the terms of the Versailles Treaty

But Italy invaded **Abyssinia** a few months later

21

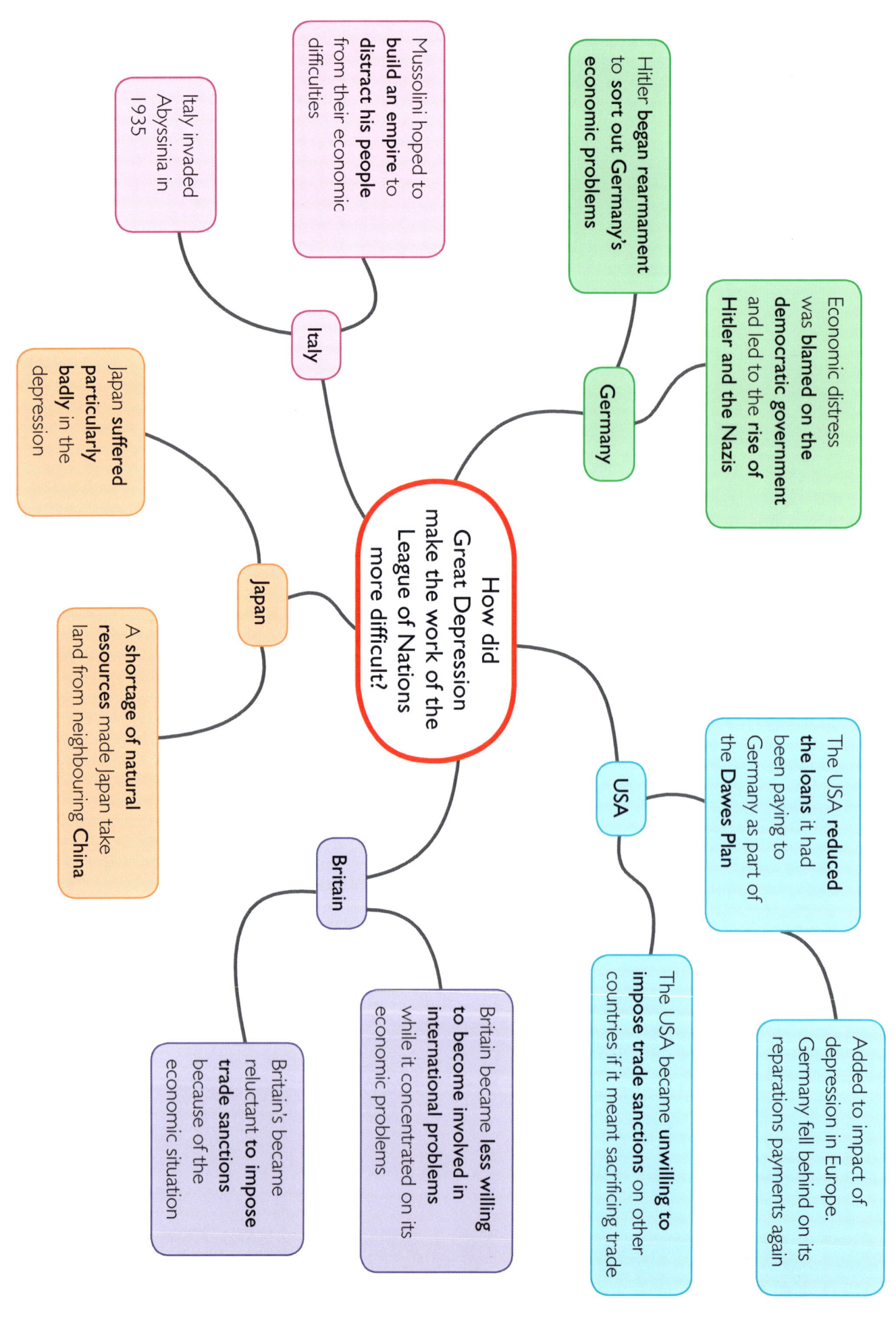

How did Great Depression make the work of the League of Nations more difficult?

Germany

Hitler began rearmament to **sort out Germany's economic problems**

Economic distress was **blamed on the democratic government** and led to the **rise of Hitler and the Nazis**

Italy

Mussolini hoped to **build an empire** to **distract his people** from their economic difficulties

Italy invaded Abyssinia in 1935

Japan

Japan **suffered particularly badly** in the depression

A **shortage of natural resources** made Japan take land from neighbouring **China**

Britain

Britain became less willing **to become involved in international problems** while it concentrated on its economic problems

Britain's became reluctant **to impose trade sanctions** because of the economic situation

USA

The USA **reduced the loans** it had been paying to Germany as part of the **Dawes Plan**

Added to impact of depression in Europe. Germany fell behind on its reparations payments again

The USA became **unwilling to impose trade sanctions** on other countries if it meant sacrificing trade

What happened during the Manchurian crisis (1931-32)? How did the League attempt to deal with the crisis?

Causes of the crisis

- Japan was **hit hard by the Great Depression**. Expansion into China was seen as a solution to economic problems
- Manchuria was a province of China containing **raw materials** that Japan needed
- Japan claimed the Chinese **sabotaged a railway in China** controlled by the Japanese
- Japan invaded Manchuria

Initial League of Nations response

- The League sent the **Lytton Commission** to investigate
- Lytton eventually reported to the League **12 months after the Japanese invasion**

The League of Nations' recommendations

- Only Japan voted against Lytton's recommendations in the League Assembly
- **Japan withdrew membership of the League** in 1933

Trade sanctions

- The League imposed **no sanctions**
- The **USA**, Japan's largest trading partner, was **not a member of the League**

Outcomes

- **Failure** for the League
- The League's **authority was seriously undermined**
- 1933: Japan invaded the remainder of China

23

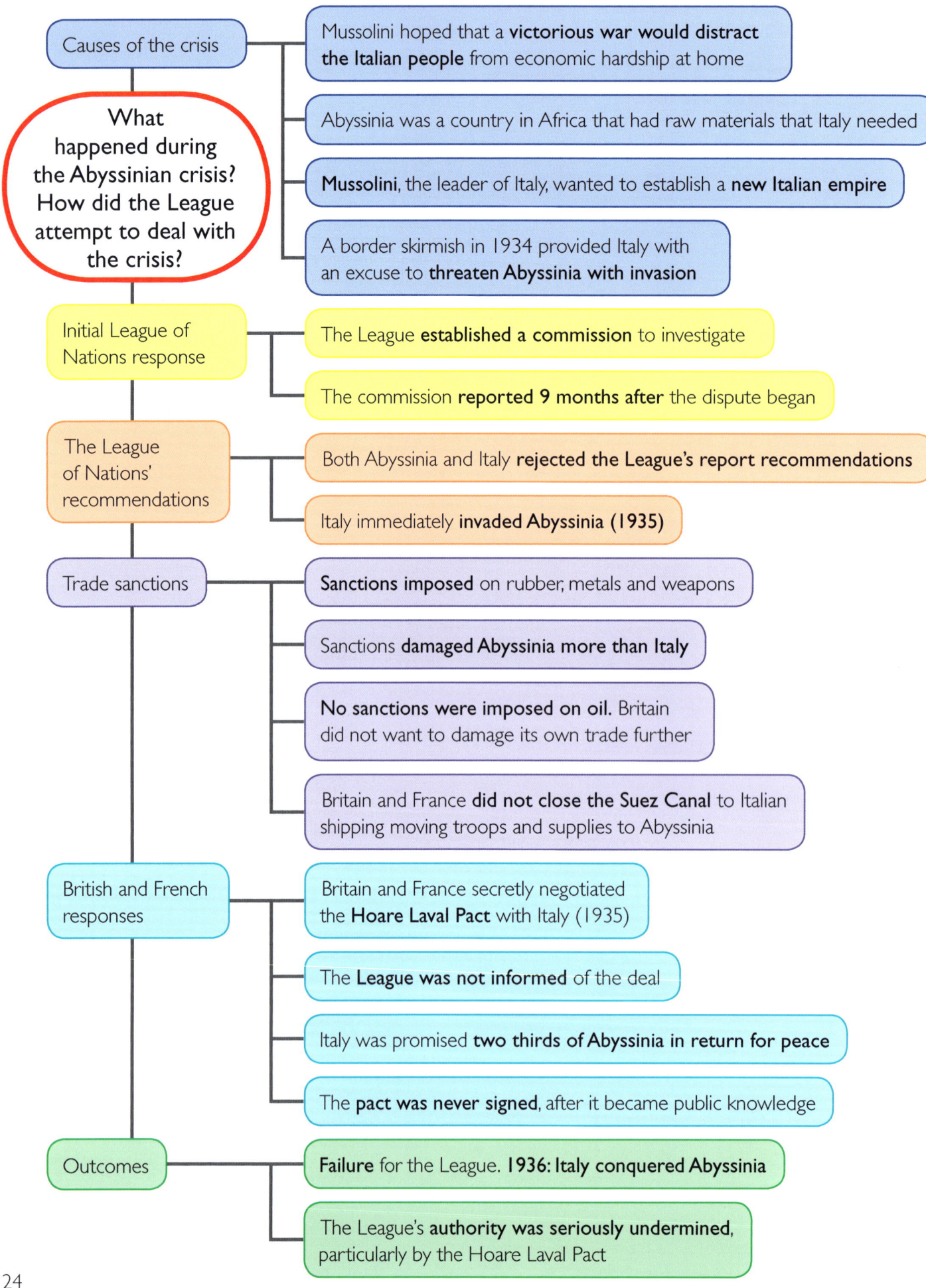

Causes of the crisis

Mussolini hoped that a **victorious war would distract the Italian people** from economic hardship at home

Abyssinia was a country in Africa that had raw materials that Italy needed

Mussolini, the leader of Italy, wanted to establish a **new Italian empire**

A border skirmish in 1934 provided Italy with an excuse to **threaten Abyssinia with invasion**

What happened during the Abyssinian crisis? How did the League attempt to deal with the crisis?

Initial League of Nations response

The League **established a commission** to investigate

The commission **reported 9 months after** the dispute began

The League of Nations' recommendations

Both Abyssinia and Italy **rejected the League's report recommendations**

Italy immediately **invaded Abyssinia (1935)**

Trade sanctions

Sanctions imposed on rubber, metals and weapons

Sanctions **damaged Abyssinia more than Italy**

No sanctions were imposed on oil. Britain did not want to damage its own trade further

Britain and France **did not close the Suez Canal** to Italian shipping moving troops and supplies to Abyssinia

British and French responses

Britain and France secretly negotiated the **Hoare Laval Pact** with Italy (1935)

The **League was not informed** of the deal

Italy was promised **two thirds of Abyssinia in return for peace**

The **pact was never signed**, after it became public knowledge

Outcomes

Failure for the League. **1936: Italy conquered Abyssinia**

The League's **authority was seriously undermined**, particularly by the Hoare Laval Pact

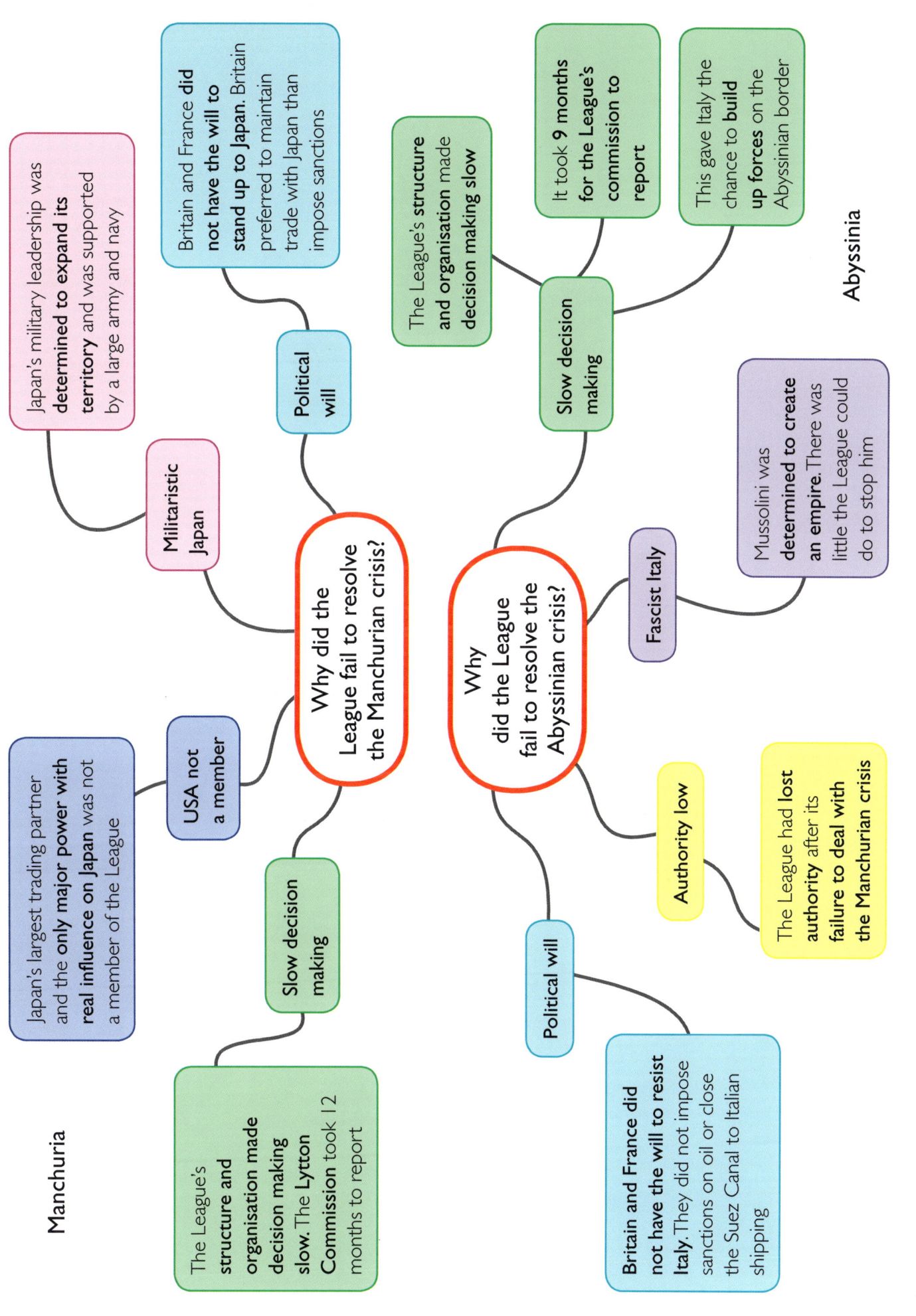

Manchuria

Why did the League fail to resolve the Manchurian crisis?

Militaristic Japan
- Japan's military leadership was **determined to expand its territory** and was supported by a large army and navy

Political will
- Britain and France **did not have the will to stand up to Japan.** Britain preferred to maintain trade with Japan than impose sanctions

USA not a member
- Japan's largest trading partner and the **only major power with real influence on Japan** was not a member of the League

Slow decision making
- The League's **structure and organisation made decision making slow.** The Lytton Commission took 12 months to report

Abyssinia

Why did the League fail to resolve the Abyssinian crisis?

Slow decision making
- The League's **structure and organisation made decision making slow**
- It took **9 months for the League's commission to report**
- This gave Italy the chance to **build up forces** on the Abyssinian border

Fascist Italy
- Mussolini was **determined to create an empire.** There was little the League could do to stop him

Authority low
- The League had **lost authority** after its failure to deal with the Manchurian crisis

Political will
- Britain and France **did not have the will to resist Italy.** They did not impose sanctions on oil or close the Suez Canal to Italian shipping

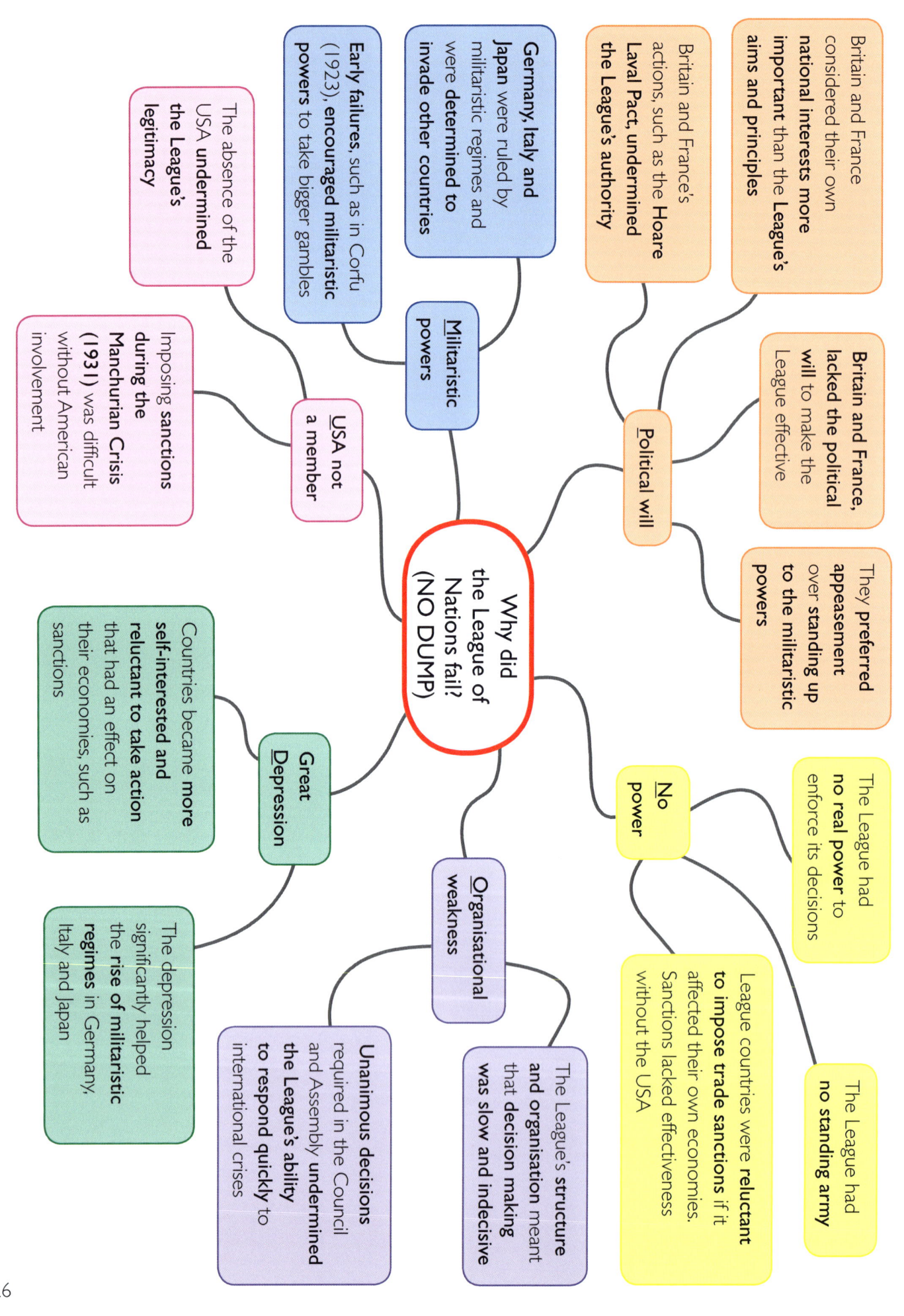

Why did the League of Nations fail? (NO DUMP)

USA not a member

- The absence of the USA undermined the League's legitimacy
- Imposing sanctions during the **Manchurian Crisis (1931)** was difficult without American involvement

Militaristic powers

- Early failures, such as in Corfu (1923), encouraged militaristic powers to take bigger gambles
- Germany, Italy and Japan were ruled by militaristic regimes and were **determined to invade other countries**

Political will

- Britain and France considered their own **national interests more important than the League's aims and principles**
- Britain and France's actions, such as the **Hoare Laval Pact, undermined the League's authority**
- **Britain and France, lacked the political will to make the League effective**
- They preferred appeasement over standing up to the militaristic powers

No power

- The League had **no real power** to enforce its decisions
- League countries were **reluctant to impose trade sanctions** if it affected their own economies. Sanctions lacked effectiveness without the USA
- The League had **no standing army**

Organisational weakness

- The League's **structure and organisation** meant that decision making was slow and indecisive
- **Unanimous decisions** required in the Council and Assembly undermined **the League's ability to respond quickly to** international crises

Great Depression

- Countries became more **self-interested and reluctant to take action** that had an effect on their economies, such as sanctions
- The depression significantly helped the **rise of militaristic regimes** in Germany, Italy and Japan

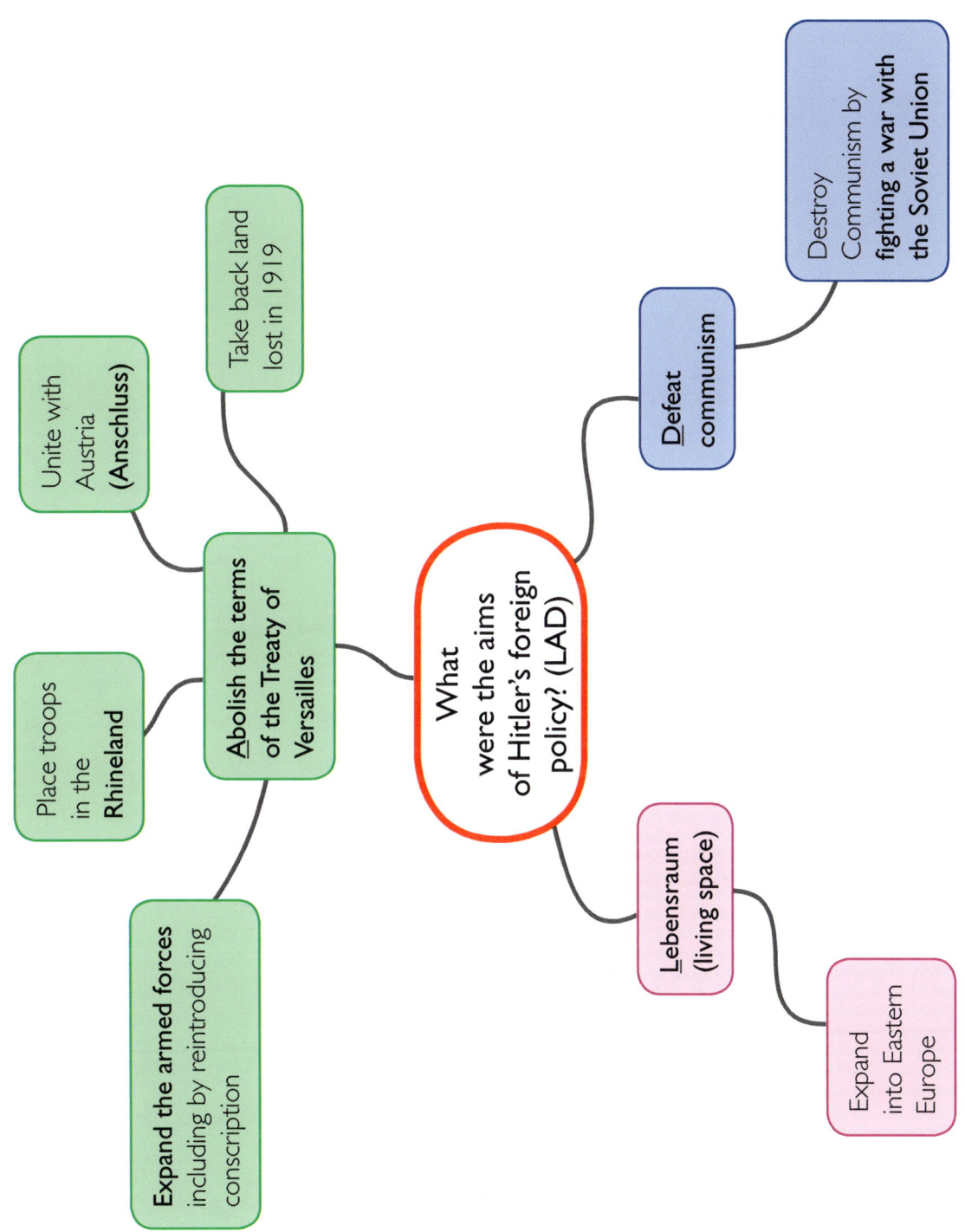

What were the aims of Hitler's foreign policy? (LAD)

Abolish the terms of the Treaty of Versailles
- Unite with Austria **(Anschluss)**
- Take back land lost in 1919
- Place troops in the **Rhineland**
- **Expand the armed forces** including by reintroducing conscription

Defeat communism
- Destroy Communism by **fighting a war with the Soviet Union**

Lebensraum (living space)
- Expand into Eastern Europe

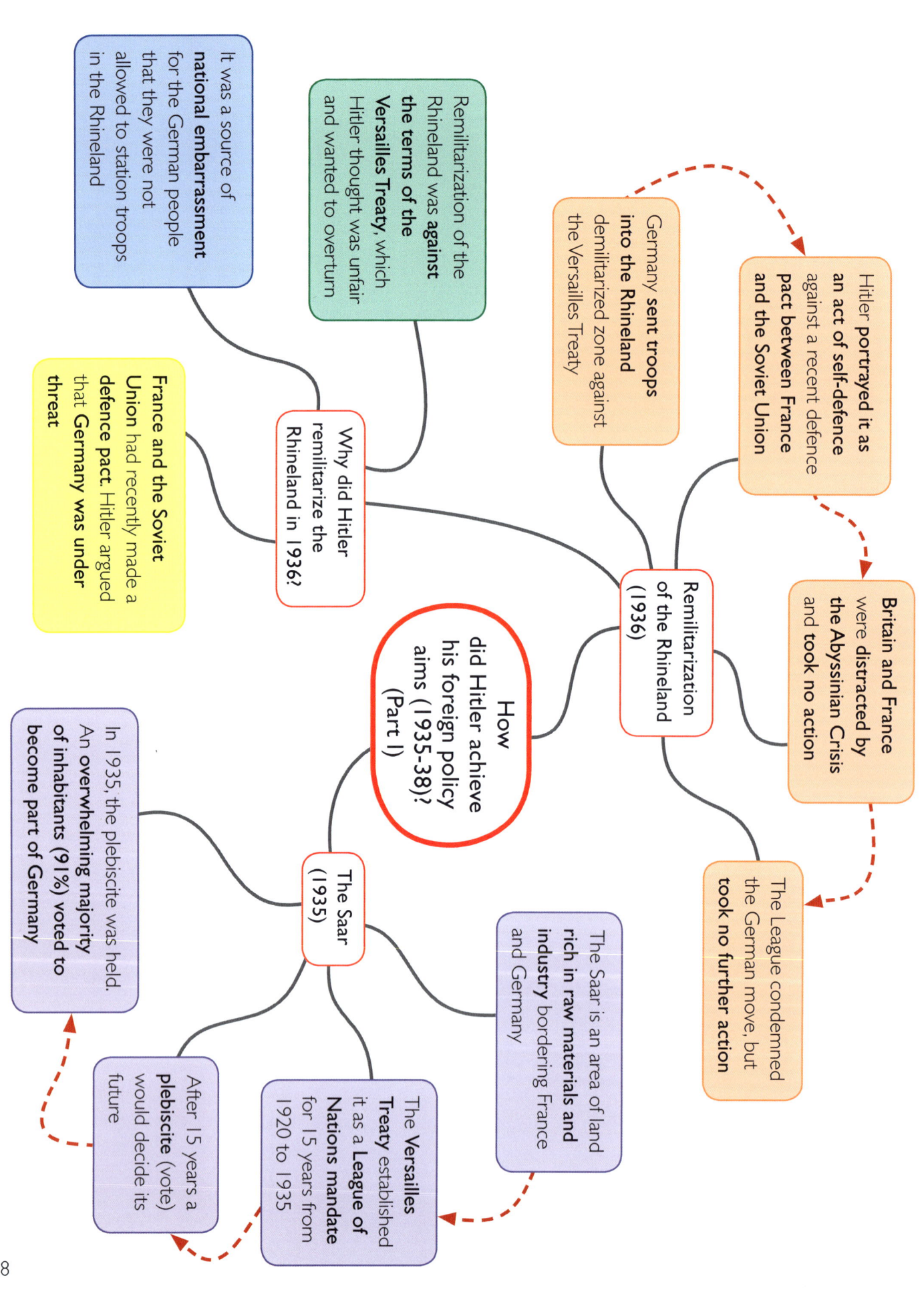

How did Hitler achieve his foreign policy aims (1935-38)? (Part I)

Why did Hitler remilitarize the Rhineland in 1936?

It was a source of **national embarrassment** for the German people that they were not allowed to station troops in the Rhineland

Remilitarization of the Rhineland was **against the terms of the Versailles Treaty,** which Hitler thought was unfair and wanted to overturn

France and the Soviet Union had recently made a **defence pact.** Hitler argued that **Germany was under threat**

Remilitarization of the Rhineland (1936)

Germany sent troops **into the Rhineland** demilitarized zone against the Versailles Treaty

Hitler portrayed it as **an act of self-defence** against a recent defence **pact between France and the Soviet Union**

Britain and France were distracted by **the Abyssinian Crisis** and took no action

The League condemned the German move, but **took no further action**

The Saar (1935)

The Saar is an area of land **rich in raw materials and industry** bordering France and Germany

The **Versailles Treaty** established it as a **League of Nations mandate** for 15 years from 1920 to 1935

After 15 years a **plebiscite** (vote) would decide its future

In 1935, the plebiscite was held. An **overwhelming majority of inhabitants (91%)** voted to become part of Germany

28

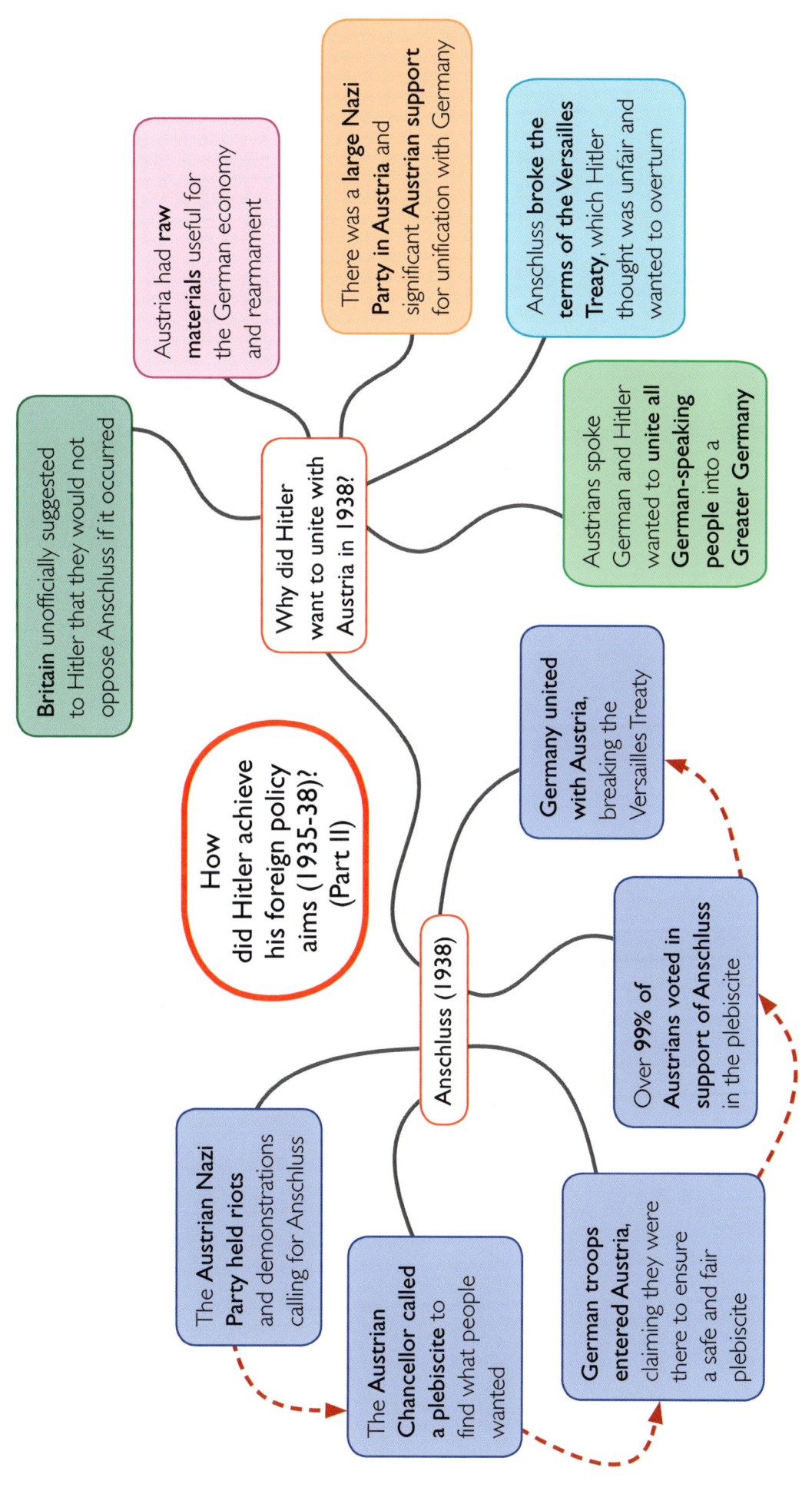

How did Hitler achieve his foreign policy aims (1935-38)? (Part II)

Why did Hitler want to unite with Austria in 1938?

Austria had **raw materials** useful for the German economy and rearmament

There was a **large Nazi Party in Austria** and significant **Austrian support** for unification with Germany

Anschluss **broke the terms of the Versailles Treaty**, which Hitler thought was unfair and wanted to overturn

Austrians spoke German and Hitler wanted to **unite all German-speaking people** into a **Greater Germany**

Britain unofficially suggested to Hitler that they would not oppose Anschluss if it occurred

Anschluss (1938)

The **Austrian Nazi Party held riots** and demonstrations calling for Anschluss

The **Austrian Chancellor called a plebiscite** to find what people wanted

German troops entered Austria, claiming they were there to ensure a safe and fair plebiscite

Over **99% of Austrians voted in support of Anschluss** in the plebiscite

Germany united with Austria, breaking the Versailles Treaty

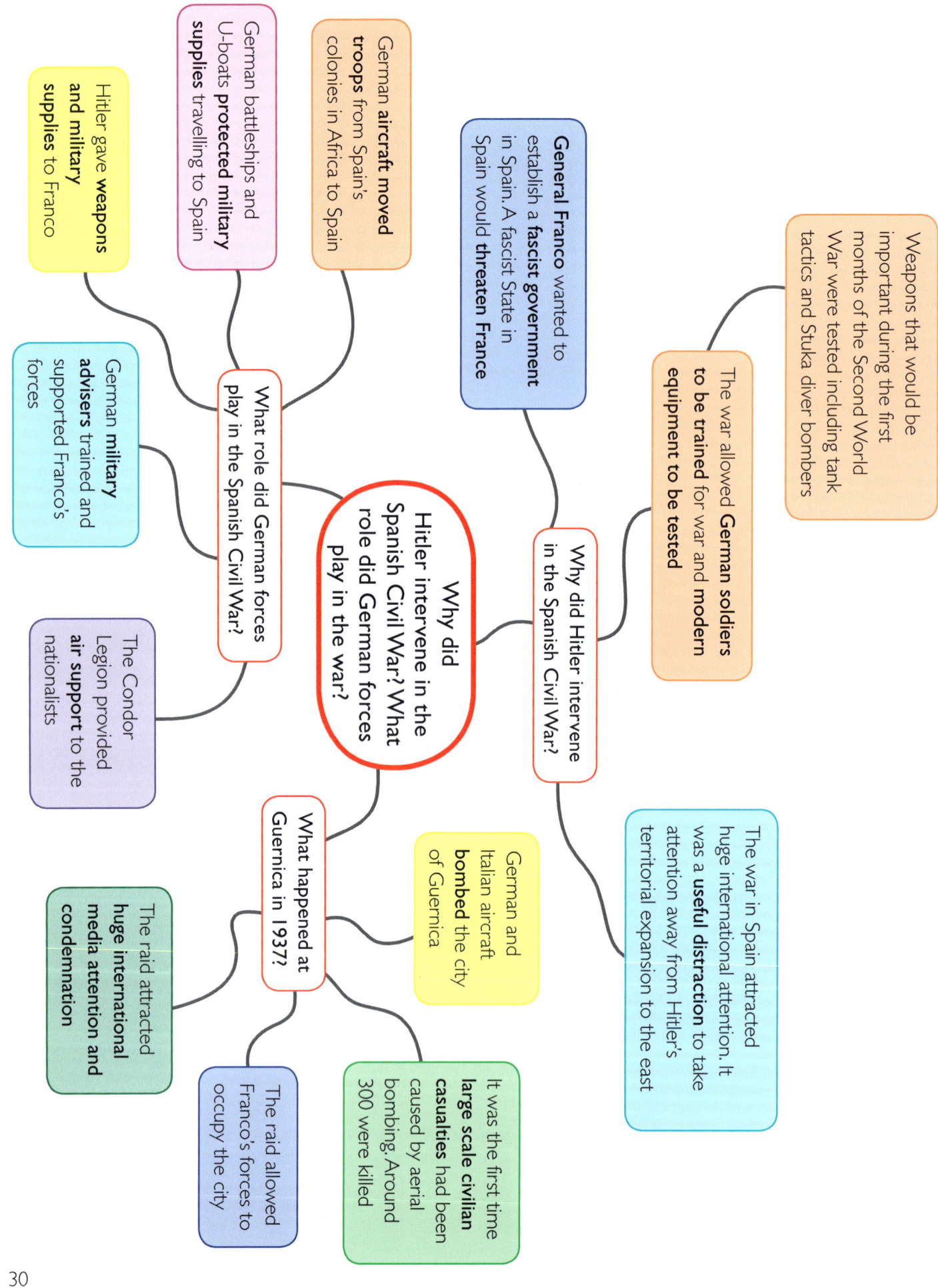

Why did Hitler intervene in the Spanish Civil War? What role did German forces play in the war?

Why did Hitler intervene in the Spanish Civil War?

General Franco wanted to establish a **fascist government** in Spain. A fascist State in Spain would **threaten France**

The war allowed **German soldiers to be trained** for war and modern **equipment to be tested**

Weapons that would be important during the first months of the Second World War were tested including tank tactics and Stuka diver bombers

The war in Spain attracted huge international attention. It was a **useful distraction** to take attention away from Hitler's territorial expansion to the east

What role did German forces play in the Spanish Civil War?

Hitler gave **weapons and military supplies** to Franco

German battleships and U-boats **protected military supplies** travelling to Spain

German **aircraft moved troops** from Spain's colonies in Africa to Spain

German **military advisers** trained and supported Franco's forces

The Condor Legion provided **air support** to the nationalists

What happened at Guernica in 1937?

German and Italian aircraft **bombed** the city of Guernica

It was the first time **large scale civilian casualties** had been caused by aerial bombing. Around 300 were killed

The raid allowed Franco's forces to occupy the city

The raid attracted **huge international media attention and condemnation**

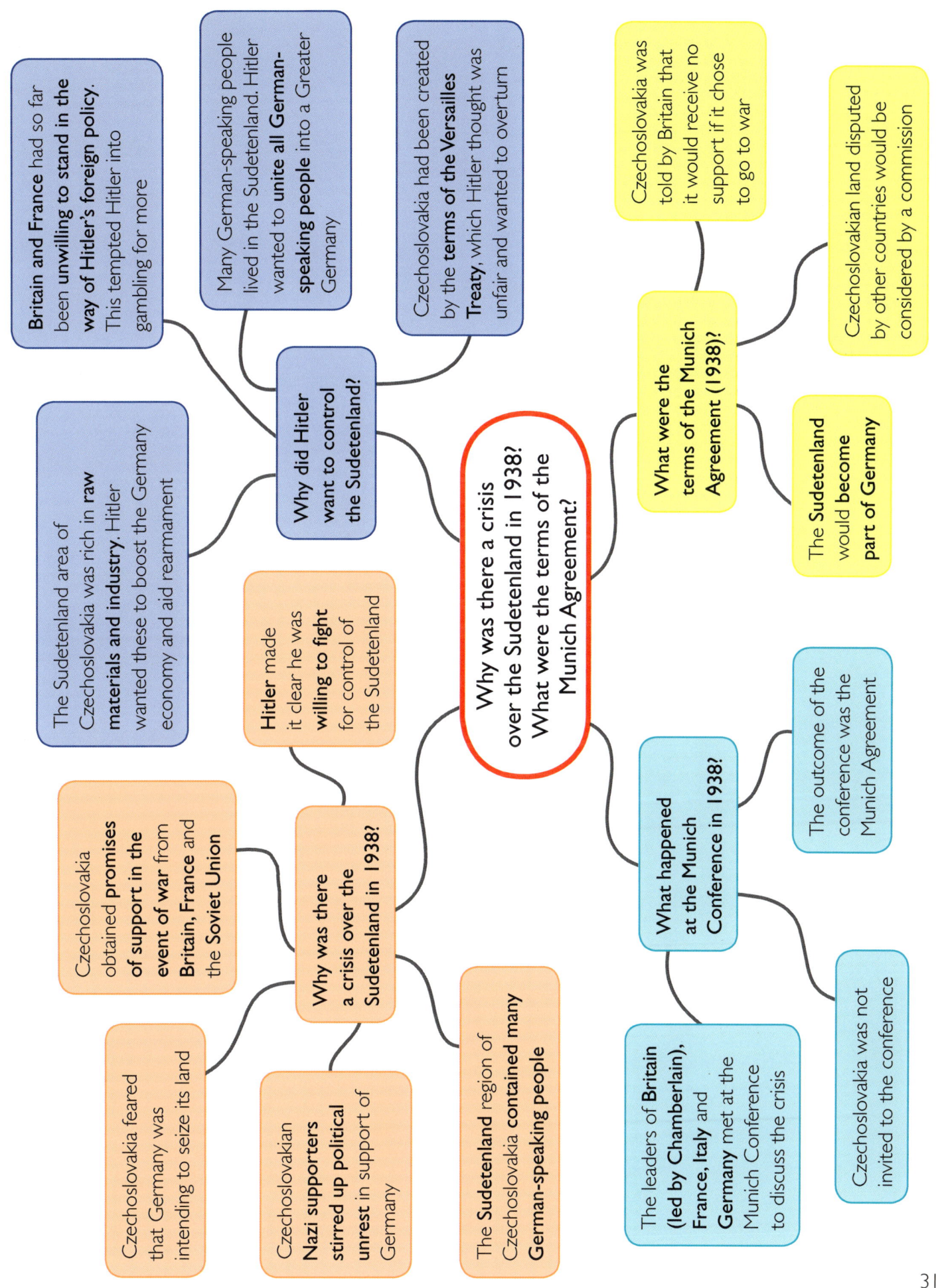

Why was there a crisis over the Sudetenland in 1938? What were the terms of the Munich Agreement?

Why did Hitler want to control the Sudetenland?

Britain and France had so far been **unwilling to stand in the way of Hitler's foreign policy.** This tempted Hitler into gambling for more

Many German-speaking people lived in the Sudetenland. Hitler wanted to **unite all German-speaking people** into a Greater Germany

Czechoslovakia had been created by the **terms of the Versailles Treaty,** which Hitler thought was unfair and wanted to overturn

The Sudetenland area of Czechoslovakia was rich in **raw materials and industry.** Hitler wanted these to boost the Germany economy and aid rearmament

What were the terms of the Munich Agreement (1938)?

Czechoslovakia was told by Britain that it would receive no support if it chose to go to war

Czechoslovakian land disputed by other countries would be considered by a commission

The Sudetenland would become **part of Germany**

Why was there a crisis over the Sudetenland in 1938?

Hitler made it clear he was **willing to fight** for control of the Sudetenland

Czechoslovakia obtained **promises of support** from **Britain, France and the Soviet Union**

Czechoslovakia feared that Germany was intending to seize its land

Czechoslovakian **Nazi supporters stirred up political unrest** in support of Germany

The **Sudetenland** region of Czechoslovakia contained many **German-speaking people**

What happened at the Munich Conference in 1938?

The outcome of the conference was the Munich Agreement

The leaders of **Britain (led by Chamberlain),** France, Italy and **Germany** met at the Munich Conference to discuss the crisis

Czechoslovakia was not invited to the conference

31

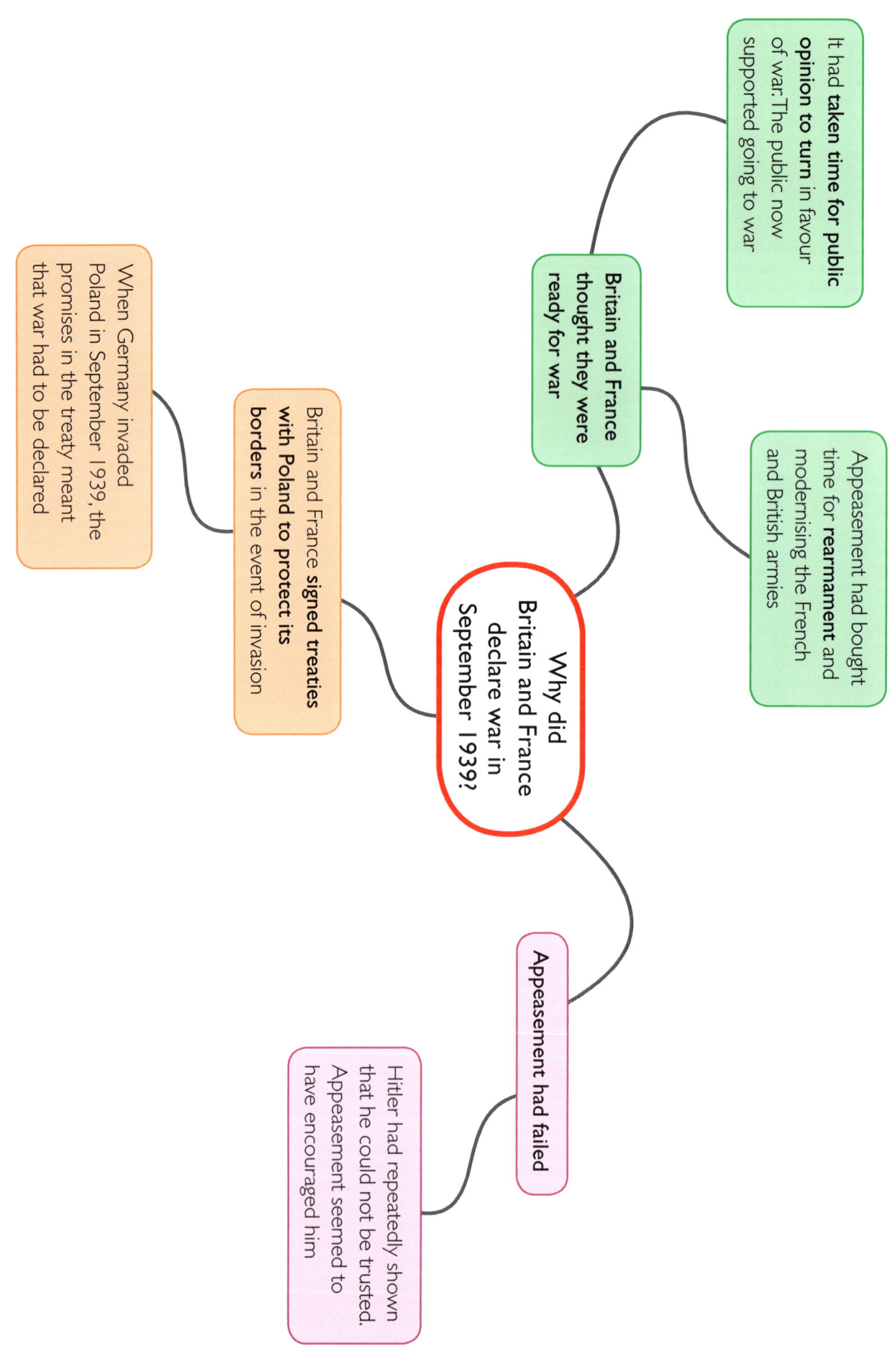

It had **taken time for public opinion to turn** in favour of war. The public now supported going to war

Appeasement had bought time for **rearmament** and modernising the French and British armies

Britain and France thought they were ready for war

Why did Britain and France declare war in September 1939?

When Germany invaded Poland in September 1939, the promises in the treaty meant that war had to be declared

Britain and France **signed treaties with Poland to protect its borders** in the event of invasion

Appeasement had failed

Hitler had repeatedly shown that he could not be trusted. Appeasement seemed to have encouraged him

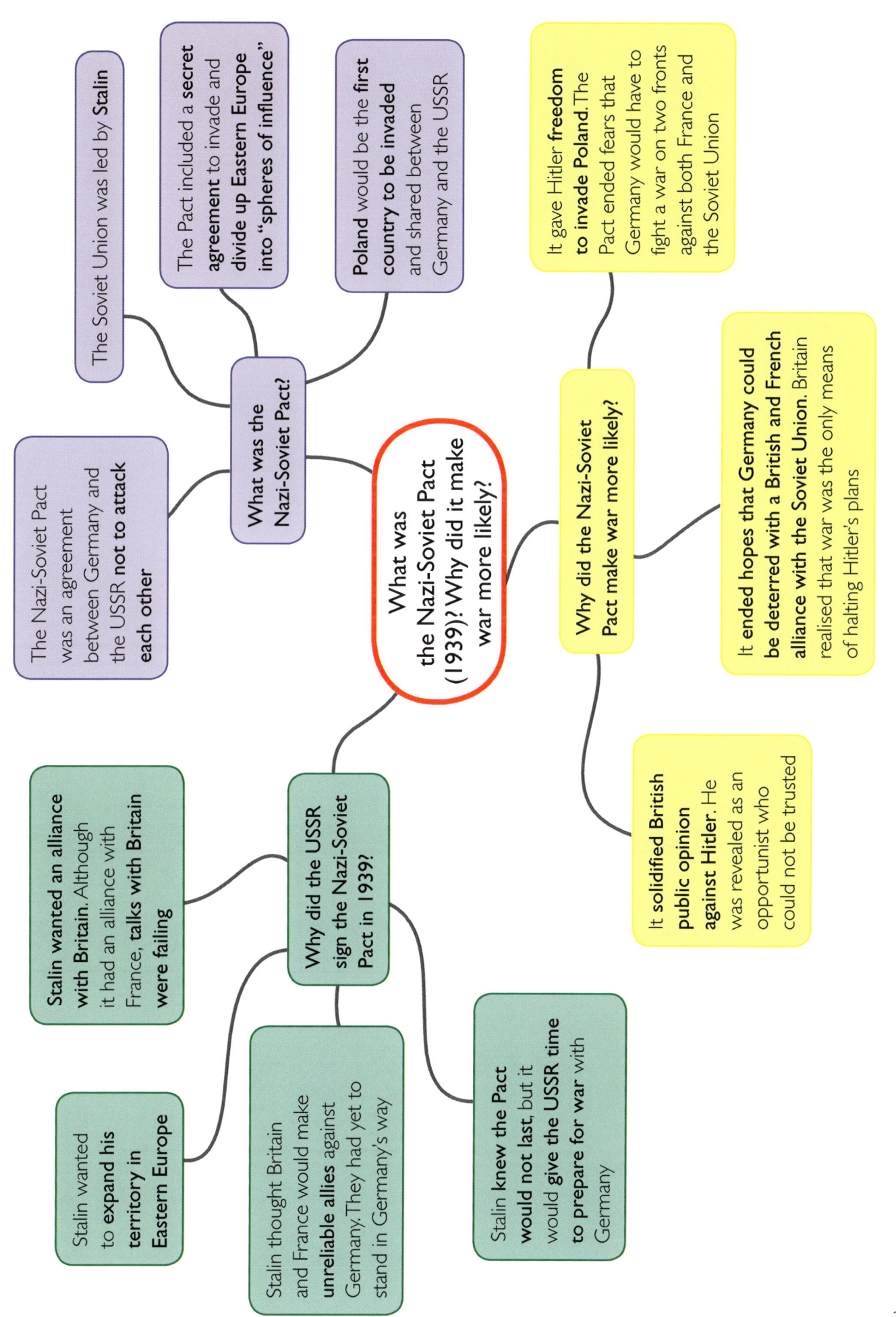

What was the Nazi-Soviet Pact (1939)? Why did it make war more likely?

What was the Nazi-Soviet Pact?

The Soviet Union was led by **Stalin**

The Pact included a **secret agreement** to invade and **divide up Eastern Europe into "spheres of influence"**

Poland would be the **first country to be invaded** and shared between Germany and the USSR

The Nazi-Soviet Pact was an agreement between Germany and the USSR **not to attack each other**

Why did the Nazi-Soviet Pact make war more likely?

It gave Hitler **freedom to invade Poland.** The Pact ended fears that Germany would have to fight a war on two fronts against both France and the Soviet Union

It ended hopes that Germany could **be deterred with a British and French alliance with the Soviet Union.** Britain realised that war was the only means of halting Hitler's plans

It **solidified British public opinion against Hitler.** He was revealed as an opportunist who could not be trusted

Why did the USSR sign the Nazi-Soviet Pact in 1939?

Stalin wanted an alliance with Britain. Although it had an alliance with France, **talks with Britain were failing**

Stalin wanted to **expand his territory in Eastern Europe**

Stalin thought Britain and France would make **unreliable allies** against Germany. They had yet to stand in Germany's way

Stalin knew the Pact would not last, but it would give the USSR time **to prepare for war** with Germany

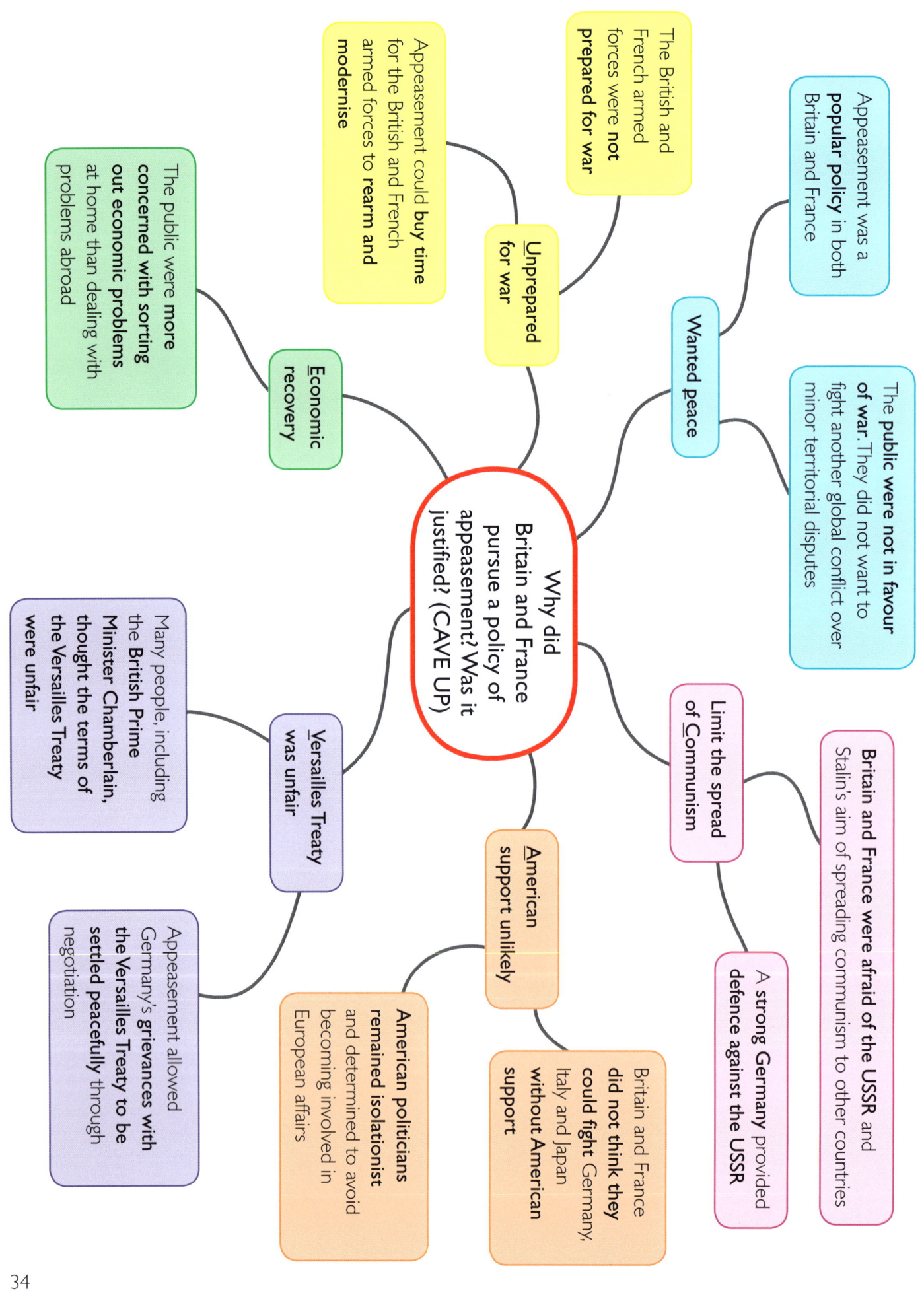

Why did Britain and France pursue a policy of appeasement? Was it justified? (CAVE UP)

Unprepared for war

The British and French armed forces were **not prepared for war**

Appeasement could **buy time** for the British and French armed forces to **rearm and modernise**

Economic recovery

The public were **more concerned with sorting out economic problems** at home than dealing with problems abroad

Wanted peace

Appeasement was a **popular policy** in both Britain and France

The public were not in favour **of war**. They did not want to fight another global conflict over minor territorial disputes

Limit the spread of Communism

Britain and France were afraid of the USSR and Stalin's aim of spreading communism to other countries

A strong Germany provided defence against the USSR

American support unlikely

American politicians remained isolationist and determined to avoid becoming involved in European affairs

Britain and France **did not think they could fight** Germany, Italy and Japan **without American support**

Versailles Treaty was unfair

Many people, including the **British Prime Minister Chamberlain, thought the terms of the Versailles Treaty** were unfair

Appeasement allowed Germany's grievances with **the Versailles Treaty to be settled peacefully** through negotiation

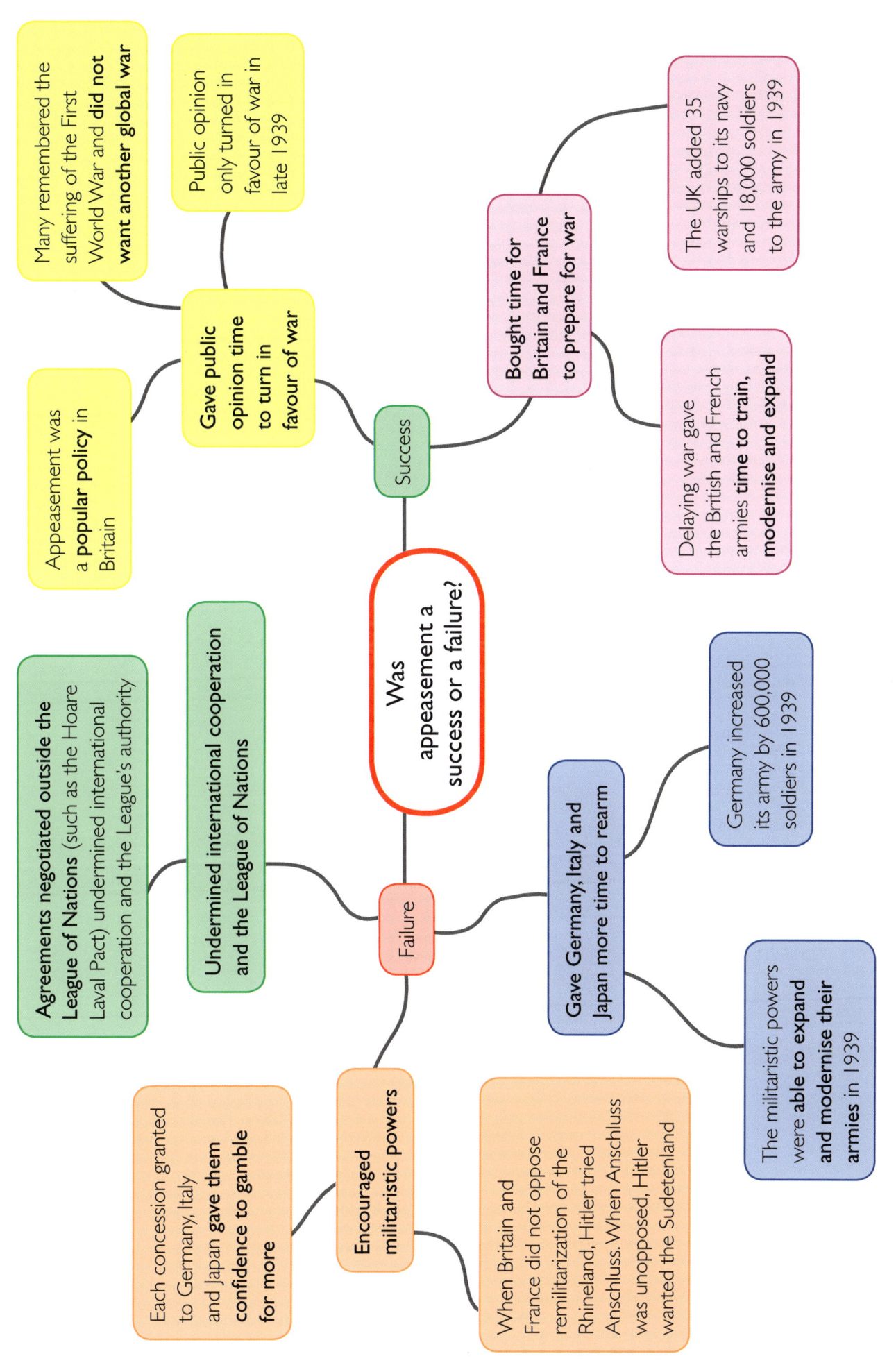

Was appeasement a success or a failure?

Success

Gave public opinion time to turn in favour of war
- Many remembered the suffering of the First World War and **did not want another global war**
- Public opinion only turned in favour of war in late 1939
- Appeasement was a **popular policy** in Britain

Bought time for Britain and France to prepare for war
- The UK added 35 warships to its navy and 18,000 soldiers to the army in 1939
- Delaying war gave the British and French armies **time to train, modernise and expand**

Failure

Agreements negotiated outside the League of Nations (such as the Hoare Laval Pact) undermined international cooperation and the League's authority

Undermined international cooperation and the League of Nations

Gave Germany, Italy and Japan more time to rearm
- Germany increased its army by 600,000 soldiers in 1939
- The militaristic powers were **able to expand and modernise their armies** in 1939

Encouraged militaristic powers
- Each concession granted to Germany, Italy and Japan **gave them confidence to gamble for more**
- When Britain and France did not oppose remilitarization of the Rhineland, Hitler tried Anschluss. When Anschluss was unopposed, Hitler wanted the Sudetenland

Revision tracking list

Track your revision by ticking off topics as you learn them.

	Little bit unsure	Fairly confident	Know it!
What were the aims and motives of Wilson (USA) at the Paris Peace Conference? What were the "14 Points"?	☐	☐	☐
What were the aims and motives of Clemenceau (France) at the Paris Peace Conference?	☐	☐	☐
What were the aims and motives of Lloyd George (Britain) at the Paris Peace Conference?	☐	☐	☐
What were the terms of the Versailles Treaty?	☐	☐	☐
What were the reasons for the terms of the Versailles Treaty?	☐	☐	☐
How satisfied was Wilson with the terms of the Versailles Treaty?	☐	☐	☐
How satisfied was Lloyd George with the terms of the Versailles Treaty?	☐	☐	☐
How satisfied was Clemenceau with the terms of the Versailles Treaty?	☐	☐	☐
How fair was the Versailles Treaty?	☐	☐	☐
How did the French react to the terms of the Versailles Treaty?	☐	☐	☐
How did Americans react to the terms of the Versailles Treaty?	☐	☐	☐
Why were the German people dissatisfied with the Versailles Treaty?	☐	☐	☐
What were the terms and consequences of the Treaty of Neuilly?	☐	☐	☐
What were the terms and consequences of the Treaty of St Germain?	☐	☐	☐
What were the terms and consequences of the Treaty of Sevres?	☐	☐	☐
What were the terms and consequences of the Treaty of Trianon?	☐	☐	☐

	Little bit unsure	Fairly confident	Know it!
Why did some countries not join the League of Nations?	☐	☐	☐
What impact did the lack of universal membership have on the League?	☐	☐	☐
What were the aims of the League of Nations?	☐	☐	☐
What was "collective security"?	☐	☐	☐
What were the structure and powers of the League of Nations?	☐	☐	☐
How successful was the League of Nations dealing with border disputes in the 1920s?	☐	☐	☐
How successful was the League of Nations dealing with social issues in the 1920s	☐	☐	☐
Why did the League of Nations have some successes dealing with border disputes in the 1920s?	☐	☐	☐
What important international agreements were agreed in the 1920s and 1930s?	☐	☐	☐
How did Great Depression make the work of the League of Nations more difficult?	☐	☐	☐
What happened during the Manchurian crisis (1931-32)?	☐	☐	☐
How did the League attempt to deal with the Manchurian crisis?	☐	☐	☐
What happened during the Abyssinian crisis?	☐	☐	☐
How did the League attempt to deal with the Abyssinian crisis?	☐	☐	☐
Why did the League fail to resolve the Manchurian crisis?	☐	☐	☐
Why did the League fail to resolve the Abyssinian crisis?	☐	☐	☐
Why did the League of Nations fail?	☐	☐	☐

	Little bit unsure	Fairly confident	Know it!
What were the aims of Hitler's foreign policy?	☐	☐	☐
What were the events of the remilitarization of the Rhineland?	☐	☐	☐
Why did Hitler remilitarize the Rhineland in 1936?	☐	☐	☐
What happened in the Saar in 1935?	☐	☐	☐
Why did Hitler intervene in the Spanish Civil War?	☐	☐	☐
What role did German forces play during the Spanish Civil War?	☐	☐	☐
What happened in the city of Guernica in 1937?	☐	☐	☐
Why did Hitler want to unite with Austria in 1938?	☐	☐	☐
How did Germany unite with Austria in 1938?	☐	☐	☐
Why did Hitler want to control the Sudetenland?	☐	☐	☐
Why was there a crisis over the Sudetenland in 1938?	☐	☐	☐
What happened at the Munich Conference in 1938?	☐	☐	☐
What were the terms of the Munich Agreement (1938)?	☐	☐	☐
Why did Britain and France declare war in September 1939?	☐	☐	☐
What was the Nazi-Soviet Pact?	☐	☐	☐
Why did the USSR sign the Nazi-Soviet Pact in 1939?	☐	☐	☐
Why did the Nazi-Soviet Pact make war more likely?	☐	☐	☐
Why did Britain and France pursue a policy of appeasement? Was it justified?	☐	☐	☐
Was appeasement a success or a failure?	☐	☐	☐

Printed in Great Britain
by Amazon

49182558R00024